Contents—Book One

Contents—Book Two

Contents—Book Three

Contents—Book Four

The Complete Guitar Player Songbook

by Russ Shipton

Omnibus Edition

Amsco Publications
New York/London/Sydney

Amsco Publications
New York/London/Sydney

Music Sales Corporation
257 Park Avenue South, New York, New York 10010 USA

Music Sales Limited
8/9 Frith Street, London W1V 5TZ England

Music Sales Pty. Limited
120 Rothschild Street, Rosebery, Sydney, NSW 2018, Australia

Order No. AM 75797
International Standard Book Number: 0.8256.2356.X

Art Direction by Mike Bell
Cover Illustration by Keith Richens
Pearce Marchbank/Howard Brown/Phil Cleaver
Arranged by Russ Shipton
Compiled by Russ Shipton

Printed in the United States of America by
Vicks Lithograph and Printing Corporation

The Complete Guitar Player Songbook

by Russ Shipton

Amsco Publications
London/New York/Sydney/Cologne

Amsco Publications
New York/London/Sydney

Music Sales Corporation
225 Park Avenue South, New York, NY 10003 USA

Music Sales Limited
8/9 Frith Street, London W1V 5TZ England

Music Sales Pty. Limited
120 Rothschild Street, Rosebery, Sydney, NSW 2018, Australia

This book Copyright © 1982 by Wise Publications.
Published 1984 by Amsco Publications,
A Division of Music Sales Corporation, New York, NY.

International Standard Book Number: 0.8256.2328.6

Art direction by Mike Bell

Printed in the United States of America by
Vicks Lithograph and Printing Corporation

Amazing Grace Traditional, arranged Russ Shipton

3/4 Rhythm/Downward Strums only

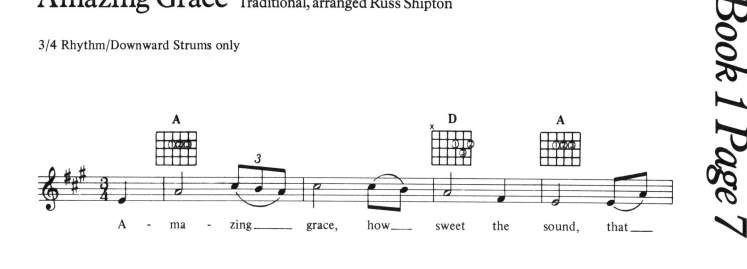

A - ma - zing _____ grace, how ___ sweet the sound, that ___

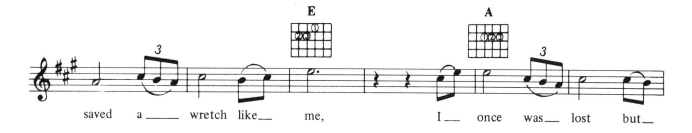

saved a _____ wretch like ___ me, I ___ once was ___ lost but ___

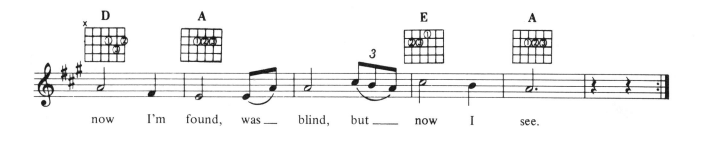

now I'm found, was ___ blind, but _____ now I see.

Verse 2:
'Twas grace that taught my heart to fear
And grace my fear relieved.
How precious did that grace appear
The hour I first believed.

Verse 3:
Through many dangers, toils and snares
We have already come.
'Twas grace that brought us safe thus far
And grace will lead us home.

Verse 4:
We've been there ten thousand years
Bright, shining as the sun.
We've no less days to sing God's praise
Than when we first begun.

Catch The Wind Donovan

3/4 Rhythm/Down and Up Strums/Mixed Patterns

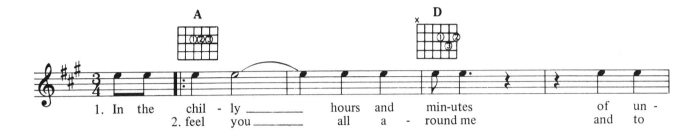

1. In the chil - ly _____ hours and min-utes of un-
2. feel you _____ all a - round me and to

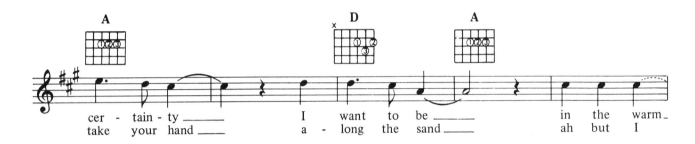

cer - tain - ty _____ I want to be _____ in the warm_
take your hand _____ a - long the sand _____ ah but I

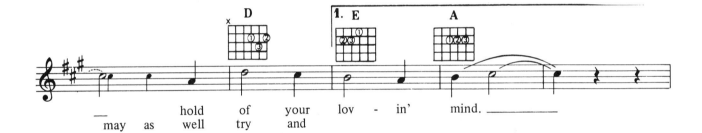

_____ may as hold of your lov - in' mind. _____
well try and

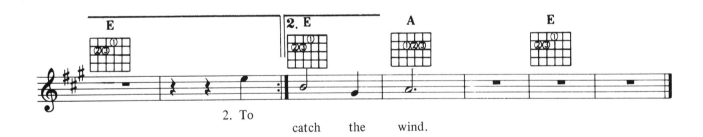

2. To catch the wind.

Verse 2:

When sundown pales the sky, I want to hide awhile behind your smile
And everywhere I'd look your eyes I'd find.
For me to love you now would be the sweetest thing, 'twould make me sing,
Ah but I may as well try and catch the wind.

Verse 3:

When rain has hung the leaves with tears, I want you near to kill my fears,
To help me to leave all my blues behind.
Standin' in your heart is where I want to be and long to be,
Ah but I may as well try and catch the wind.

4

Leaving On A Jet Plane   John Denver

4/4 Rhythm/Down strums only

Verse 2:
There's so many times I've let you down, so many times I've played around,
I tell you now, they don't mean a thing.
Every place I go I'll think of you, every song I sing I'll sing for you
When I come back, I'll wear your wedding ring.

Verse 3:
Well now the time has come to leave you, one more time please let me kiss you,
Then close your eyes and I'll be on my way.
Dream about the days to come, when I won't have to leave you alone
About the times I won't have to say:

Blowin' In The Wind Bob Dylan

4/4 Rhythm/Down and Up Strums/One Pattern only

VERSE

How man-y roads must a man walk down be-fore you call him a

man? Yes 'n how man-y seas must the white dove sail, be-fore she

sleeps in the sand? Yes 'n how man-y times must the can-non balls fly, be-

CHORUS

fore they're for-ev-er banned? The ans-wer my friend, is

blow-in' in the wind, the ans-wer is blow-in' in the wind.

Verse 2:
How many times must a man look up, before he can see the sky?
Yes'n how many ears must one man have, before he can hear people cry?
Yes'n how many deaths will it take till he knows, that too many people have died?

Verse 3:
How many years can a mountain exist, before it is washed to the sea?
Yes'n how many years can some people exist, before they're allowed to be free?
Yes'n how many times can a man turn his head, pretending that he just doesn't see?

6

The Times They Are A-Changin' Bob Dylan

3/4 Rhythm/Bass-Strum/Mixed Patterns

Come ga-ther round peo-ple, wher-ev-er you roam ____ and ad-mit that the wa-ters a-round you have grown, and ac-cept it that soon you'll be drenched to the bone ____ if your time to you is worth sav-in', ____ then you'd bet-ter start swimmin' or you'll sink like a stone, for the times they are a-chang - in'! ____ (Come)

Verse 2:
Come writers and critics who prophesies with your pen,
And keep your eyes wide, the chance won't come again,
And don't speak too soon for the wheel's still in spin,
And there's no tellin' who that it's namin',
For the loser now will be later to win,
For the times they are a-changin'.

Verse 3:
Come senators, congressmen, please heed the call
Don't stand in the doorway, don't block up the hall.
For he that gets hurt will be he who has stalled.
There's a battle outside and it's ragin'.
It'll soon shake your windows and rattle your walls
For the times they are a-changin'.

Verse 4:
Come mothers and fathers throughout the land,
And don't criticise what you can't understand.
Your sons and your daughters are beyond your command,
Your old road is rapidly agin'.
Please get out of the new one if you can't lend your hand
For the times they are a-changin'.

Verse 5:
The line it is drawn the curse it is cast.
The slow one now will later be fast.
As the present now will later be past
The order is rapidly fadin'.
And the first one now will later be last
For the times they are a-changin'.

Colours Donovan

4/4 Rhythm/Bass-Strum/Downstrokes only

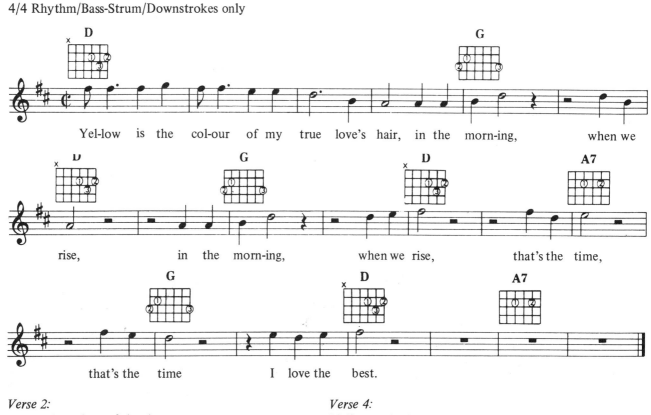

Yel-low is the col-our of my true love's hair, in the morn-ing, when we

rise, in the morn-ing, when we rise, that's the time,

that's the time I love the best.

Verse 2:
Blue is the colour of the sky
In the morning, when we rise,
In the morning, when we rise,
That's the time, that's the time
I love the best.

Verse 3:
Green is the colour of the sparklin' corn
In the morning, when we rise,
In the morning, when we rise,
That's the time, that's the time
I love the best.

Verse 4:
Mellow is the feelin' that I get
When I see her, mm hmm,
When I see her, uh huh,
That's the time, that's the time
I love the best.

Verse 5:
Freedom is a word I rarely use
Without thinkin', mm hmm,
Without thinkin', mm hmm
Of the time, of the time
When I've been loved.

Me and Bobby McGee Kris Kristofferson

4/4 Rhythm Bass-Strum/Down and Up Strokes/One Pattern only

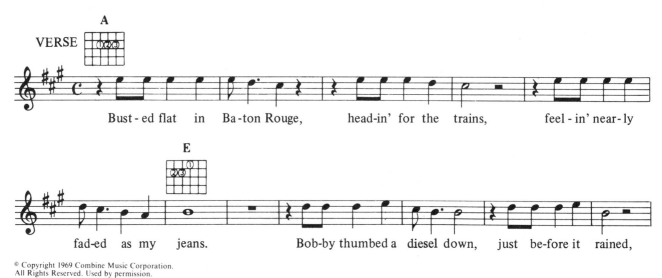

VERSE

Bust-ed flat in Ba-ton Rouge, head-in' for the trains, feel-in' near-ly

fad-ed as my jeans. Bob-by thumbed a diesel down, just be-fore it rained,

8

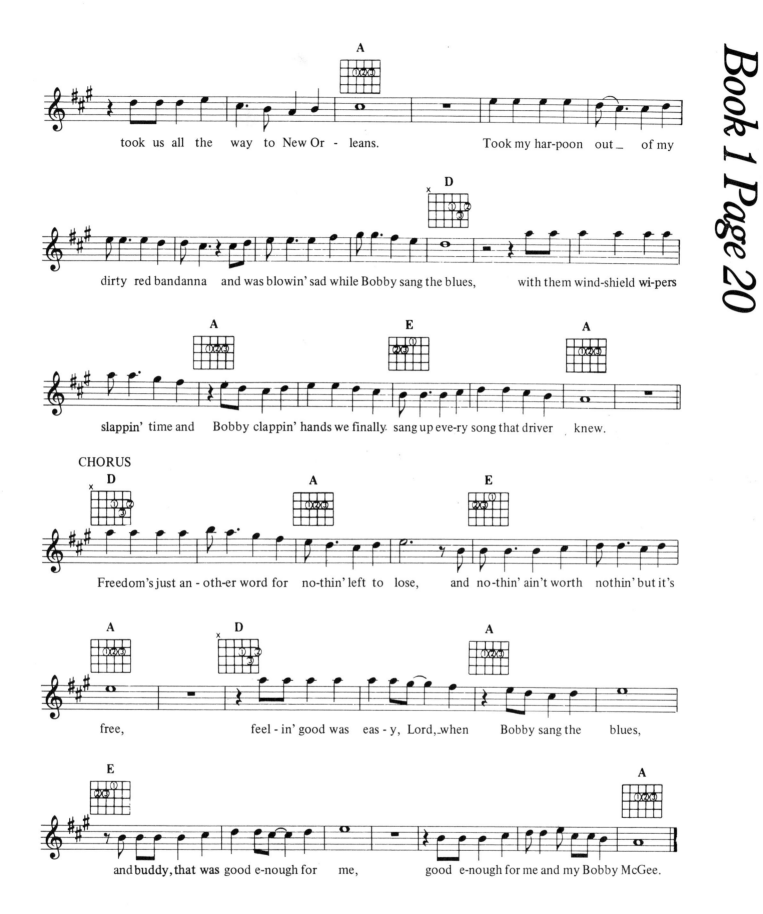

took us all the way to New Or - leans. Took my har-poon out of my

dirty red bandanna and was blowin' sad while Bobby sang the blues, with them wind-shield wi-pers

slappin' time and Bobby clappin' hands we finally sang up eve-ry song that driver knew.

CHORUS

Freedom's just an - oth-er word for no-thin' left to lose, and no-thin' ain't worth nothin' but it's

free, feel - in' good was eas - y, Lord, when Bobby sang the blues,

and buddy, that was good e-nough for me, good e-nough for me and my Bobby McGee.

Verse 2:

From the coalmines of Kentucky to the California sun, Bobby shared the secrets of my soul,
Standin' right beside me through everythin' I done, and every night she kept me from the cold.
Then somewhere near Selinas, Lord, I let slip away, she was lookin' for the love I hoped she'd find,
Well I'd trade all my tomorrows for a single yesterday, holdin' Bobby's body close to mine.

2nd chorus:

Freedom's just another word for nothin' left to lose, and nothin' left was all she left for me,
Feelin' good was easy Lord, when Bobby sang the blues, and buddy that was good enough for me.
Good enough for me and Bobby McGee.

Scarborough Fair   Traditional, arranged Russ Shipton

3/4 Rhythm/Arpeggio/One Pattern only

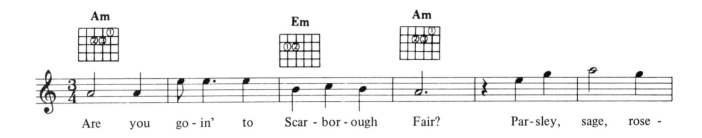

Are   you   go - in'   to   Scar - bor - ough   Fair?   Par - sley,   sage,   rose -

ma - ry__ and   thyme.   Re - mem - ber   me   to the   one   who   lives

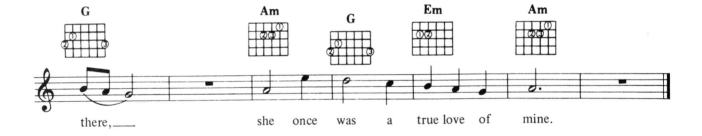

there,___   she   once   was   a   true love   of   mine.

Verse 2:
Tell her to make me a cambric shirt:
Parsley, sage, rosemary and thyme;
Without any seams nor needle work,
Then she'll be a true love of mine.

Verse 3:
Tell her to find me an acre of land:
Parsley, sage; rosemary and thyme;
Between the salt water and the sea strand,
Then she'll be atrue love of mine.

Verse 4:
Tell her to plough it with sickle of leather.
Parsley, sage, rosemary and thyme;
And bind it all in a bunch of heather,
Then she'll be a true love of mine.

English Country Garden R M Jordan

4/4 Rhythm/Arpeggio/Single Pattern only

How man-y gen-tle flo-wers grow in an Eng-lish coun-try ga-ar - den?

I'll tell you now of some that I know and those I miss you'll sure - ly par - don.

Daf-fo-dils, heart's ease and flocks, meadow sweet and lil-ies stocks gentle lupin and tall hol-ly- hocks, roses

fox-gloves, snowdrops, forget-me-nots, in an Eng-lish coun-try ga-ar-den.

Verse 2:
How many insects find their home in an English country garden?
I'll tell you now of some that I know and those I miss you'll surely pardon.
Dragonflies, moths and bees, spiders falling from the trees
Butterflies sway in the mild, gentle breeze,
There are hedgehogs that roam and little gnomes, in an English country garden.

Verse 3:
How many songbirds make their nests in an English country garden?
I'll tell you now of some that I know and those I miss you'll surely pardon.
Babbling coo, cooing doves, robins and the warbling thrush
Bluebird, lark, finch and nightingale.
We all smile in the spring, when the birds all start to sing
In an English country garden.

11

The Last Thing On My Mind Tom Paxton

4/4 Rhythm/Arpeggio/Two Possible Patterns

Verse 2:
You've got reason a-plenty for going, this I know, this I know
For the weeds have been steadily growing, please don't go, please don't go.

Verse 3:
As I lie in my bed in the morning, without you, without you
Each song in my breast dies a-borning, without you, without you.

Verse 4:
As I walk down the street the subway's rumbling underground, underground
While the thoughts in my head they're a-tumbling round and round, round and round.

Yellow Submarine Lennon/McCartney

4/4 Rhythm/Swing Pattern Strumming

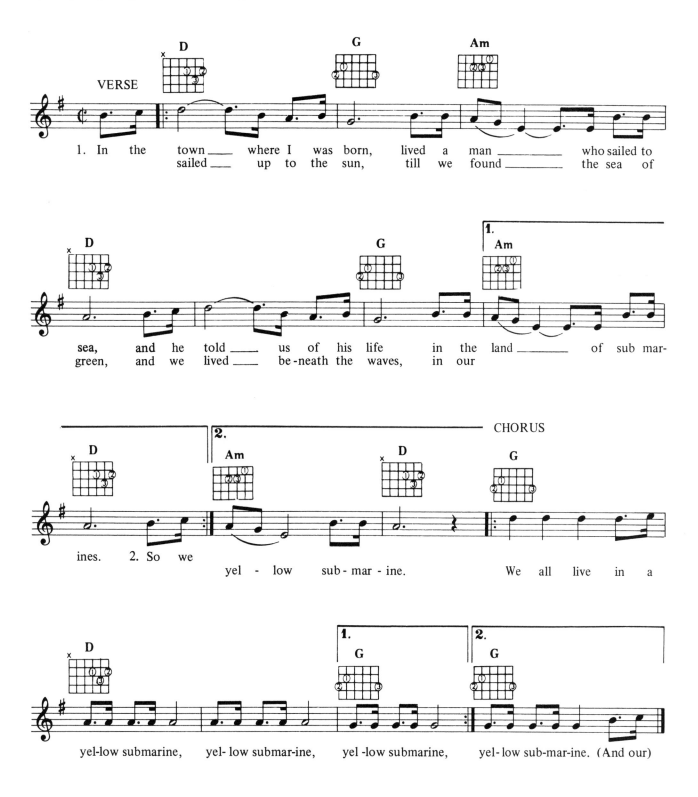

VERSE

1. In the town _____ where I was born, lived a man _____ who sailed to
   sailed _____ up to the sun, till we found _____ the sea of

sea, and he told _____ us of his life in the land _____ of sub mar-
green, and we lived _____ be-neath the waves, in our

ines. 2. So we

yel - low sub - mar - ine. We all live in a

CHORUS

yel-low submarine, yel-low submar-ine, yel-low submarine, yel-low sub-mar-ine. (And our)

Verse 3:
And our friends are all on board, many more of them live next door
And the band begins to play . . . .

Verse 4:
As we live a life of ease, everyone of us has all we need
Sky of blue, sea of green, in our yellow submarine.

Maxwell's Silver Hammer Lennon/McCartney

4/4 Rhythm/Swing Strum Patterns Mixed/Stops

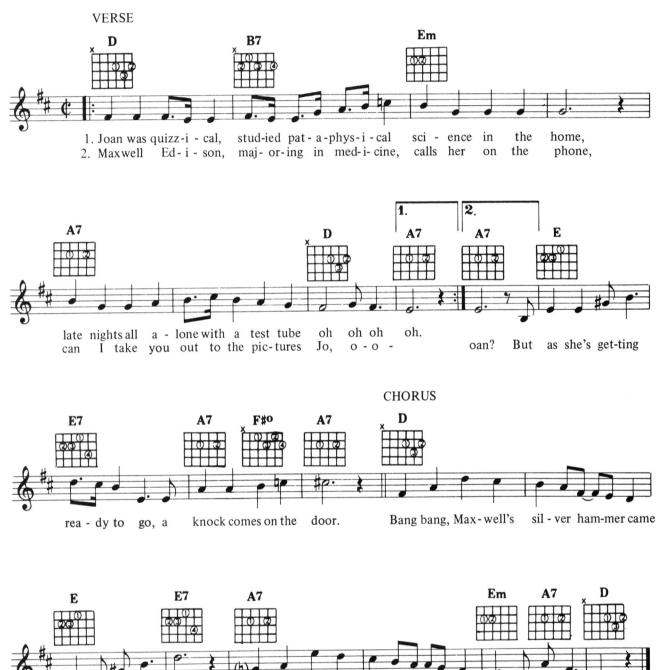

VERSE

D   B7   Em

1. Joan was quizz-i - cal, stud-ied pat-a-phys-i-cal sci - ence in the home,
2. Maxwell Ed-i-son, maj-or-ing in med-i-cine, calls her on the phone,

A7   D   1. A7   2. A7   E

late nights all a - lone with a test tube oh oh oh oh.
can I take you out to the pic-tures Jo, o - o - oan? But as she's get-ting

CHORUS

E7   A7   F#o   A7   D

rea - dy to go, a knock comes on the door.   Bang bang, Max-well's sil - ver ham-mer came

E   E7   A7   Em   A7   D

down up on her head.   Clang, clang, Maxwell's sil-ver hammer made sure that she was dead.

Verse 2:
Back in school again, Maxwell plays the fool again, teacher gets annoyed,
Wishing to avoid an unpleasant scee - e - ene.
She tells Max to stay when the class has gone away so he waits behind
Writing fifty times "I must not be so - o - o - o".
But when she turns her back on the boy, he creeps up from behind . . . .

Verse 3:
P.C. Thirty-One said "We've caught a dirty one", Maxwell stands alone
Painting testimonial pictures, oh, oh, oh, oh.
Rose and Valerie, screaming from the gallery, say "He must go free".
The judge does not agree and he tells them so - o - o - o.
But as the words are leaving his lips, a noise comes from behind . . . .

Ob-la-di Ob-la-da Lennon/McCartney

4/4 Rhythm/Continuous Down/Up Strum/One Pattern only

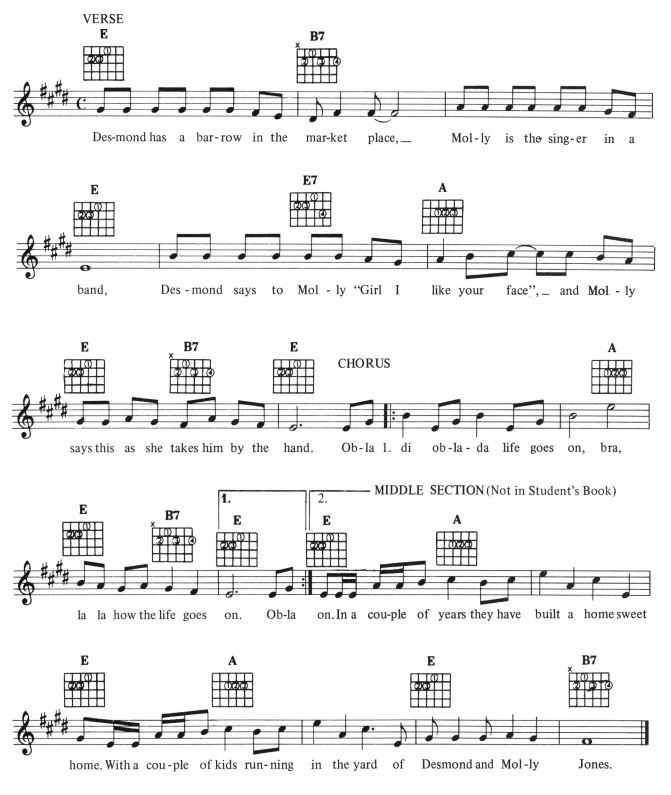

Verse 2:
Desmond takes a trolley to the jeweller's store, buys a twenty carat golden ring,
Takes it back to Molly waiting at the door, and as he gives it to her she begins to sing:
"Ob-la-di, ob-la-da life goes on, bra, la la how the life goes on *(rpt.)*.

Verse 3:
Happy ever after in the market place, Desmond lets the children lend a hand
Molly stays at home and does her pretty face and in the evening she still sings it with the band:
"Ob-la-di, ob-la-da life goes on, bra, la la how the life goes on *(rpt.)*.

Drunken Sailor Traditional, arranged Russ Shipton

4/4 Rhythm/Bass-Strum with Hammer-ons

VERSE **Dm** **C**

What shall we do with the drun-ken sai - lor? What shall we do with the drun-ken sai - lor?

Dm **C** **Dm**

What shall we do with the drun-ken sai - lor, ear - lye in the morn - ing?

CHORUS **C**

Wey, hey, and up she ris - es, wey hey, and up she ris - es,

Dm **C** **Dm**

Wey, hey, and up she ris - es, ear - lye in the morn - ing.

Verse 2:
Put him in the scuppers with a hose-pipe on him *(x 3)*
Earlye in the morning.

Verse 4:
Tie him by the legs in a running bowline *(x 3)*
Earlye in the morning.

Verse 3:
Put him in the longboat until he's sober *(x 3)*
Earlye in the morning.

This Land Is Your Land Woody Guthrie

4/4 Rhythm Mixed Bass-Strum Patterns/Bass Runs

VERSE/ **G** **C** **G**
CHORUS

This land is your land, this land is my land, from Cal - i -

D **G** **C**

for - nia to the New York is - land, from the red - wood for - ests,

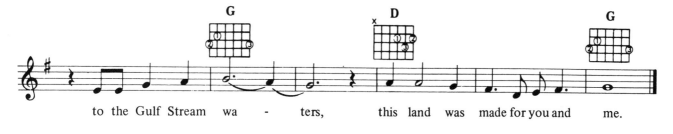

to the Gulf Stream wa - ters, this land was made for you and me.

Verse 2:
As I went walking that ribbon of highway
I saw above me that endless skyway
I saw below me that golden valley
This land was made for you and me.

Verse 3:
I roamed and rambled and I followed my footsteps
To the sparkling sands of her diamond deserts.
All around me a voice was sounding
This land was made for you and me.

Verse 4:
When the sun came shining, then I was strolling
And the wheat fields waving, and the dust clouds rolling.
A voice was chanting, as the fog was lifting
This land was made for you and me.

The House Of The Risin' Sun Traditional, arranged Russ Shipton

3/4 Rhythm/Arpeggio/Mixed Patterns

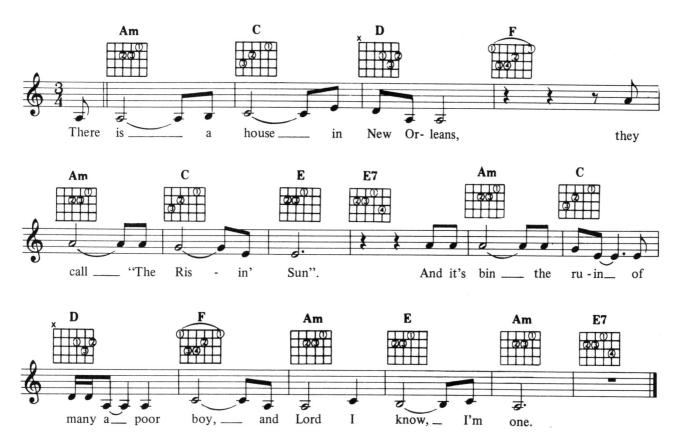

There is ____ a house ____ in New Or- leans, they

call ____ "The Ris - in' Sun". And it's bin ____ the ru-in____ of

many a__ poor boy, ____ and Lord I know, __ I'm one.

Verse 2:
My mother was a tailor, sewed my new blue jeans.
My father was a gamblin' man, down in New Orleans.

Verse 3:
Now the only thing to gamblin' is a suitcase and a trunk
And the only time he's satisfied is when he's on a drunk.

Verse 4:
Go tell my baby sister not to do what I have done
To shun that house in New Orleans, they call "The Risin' Sun".

Verse 5:
One foot on the platform, the other's on the train
I'm goin' back to New Orleans, to wear that ball and chain.

Sailing   G. Sutherland

4/4 Rhythm/Arpeggio with Hammer-ons, Bass Run and Stop

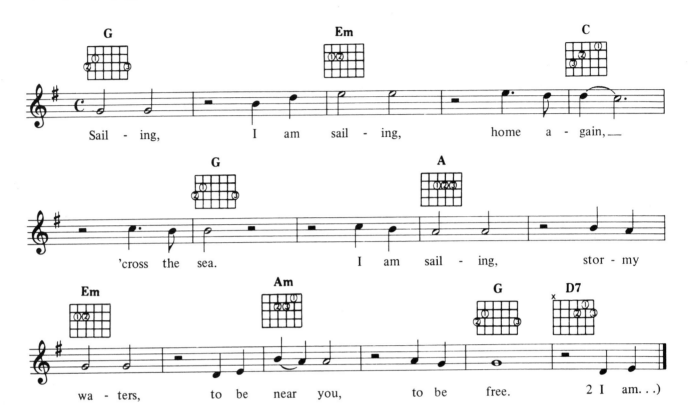

Sail - ing, I am sail - ing, home a - gain, __ 'cross the sea. I am sail - ing, stor - my wa - ters, to be near you, to be free. 2 I am. . .)

Verse 2:
I am flying, I am flying, like a bird, 'cross the sky,
I am flying, passing high clouds, to be with you, to be free.

Verse 3:
Can you hear me? Can you hear me? Through the dark night, far away.
I am dying, forever trying, to be with you, who can say?

Freight Train   James and Williams

4/4 Rhythm/Single Alternating Thumb Pattern

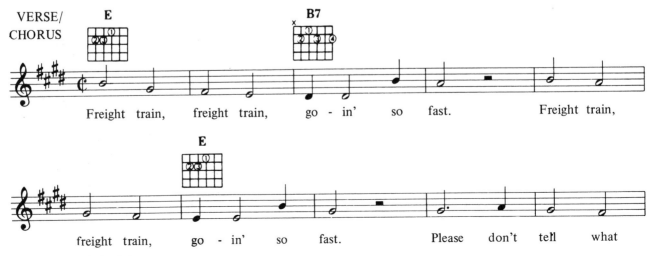

Freight train, freight train, go - in' so fast. Freight train, freight train, go - in' so fast. Please don't tell what

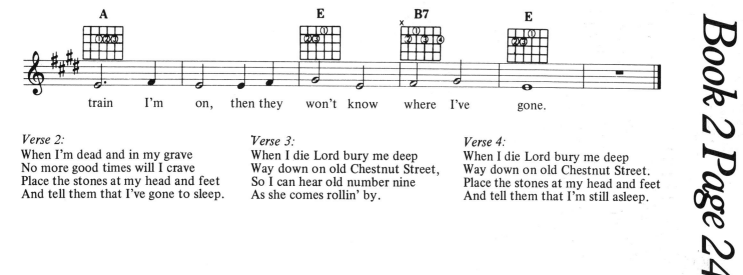

train I'm on, then they won't know where I've gone.

Verse 2:
When I'm dead and in my grave
No more good times will I crave
Place the stones at my head and feet
And tell them that I've gone to sleep.

Verse 3:
When I die Lord bury me deep
Way down on old Chestnut Street,
So I can hear old number nine
As she comes rollin' by.

Verse 4:
When I die Lord bury me deep
Way down on old Chestnut Street.
Place the stones at my head and feet
And tell them that I'm still asleep.

If I Were A Carpenter Tim Hardin

4/4 Rhythm/Alternating Thumb/One Pattern only

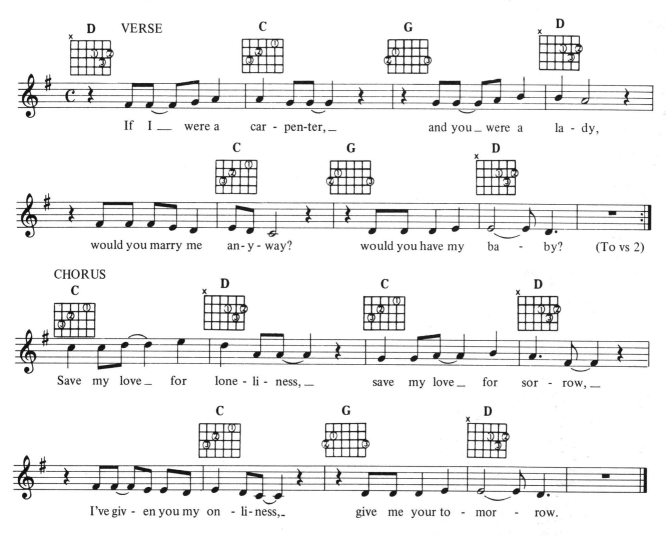

VERSE
If I __ were a car-pen-ter, __ and you __ were a la-dy,
would you marry me an-y-way? would you have my ba — by? (To vs 2)

CHORUS
Save my love __ for lone-li-ness, __ save my love __ for sor-row, __
I've giv-en you my on-li-ness, __ give me your to-mor-row.

Verse 2:
If a tinker were my trade, would you still find me
Carrying the pots I made, following behind me?

Verse 4:
If I worked my hands in wood, would you still love me?
Answer me, babe, "Yes I would, I'd place you above me".

Verse 3:
If I were a miller, at my mill wheel grinding,
Would you miss your coloured blouse, and your soft shoes shining?

Study Fernando Sor

4/4 Rhythm/Simple Classical Style

Moon Shadow Cat Stevens

4/4 Rhythm/Strumming/Mixed Patterns

CHORUS

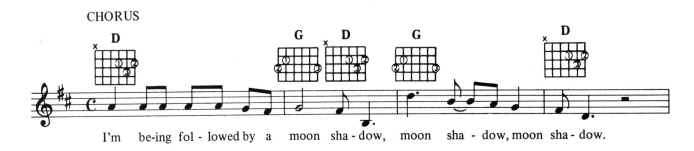

I'm be-ing fol-lowed by a moon sha-dow, moon sha-dow, moon sha-dow.

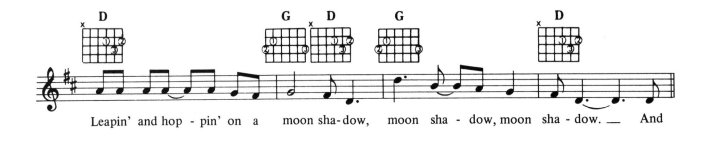

Leapin' and hop-pin' on a moon sha-dow, moon sha-dow, moon sha-dow. __ And

VERSE

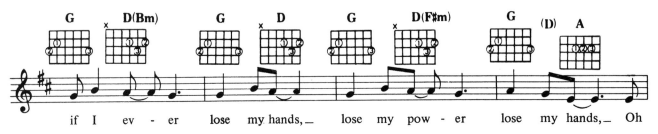

if I ev-er lose my hands, __ lose my pow-er lose my hands, __ Oh

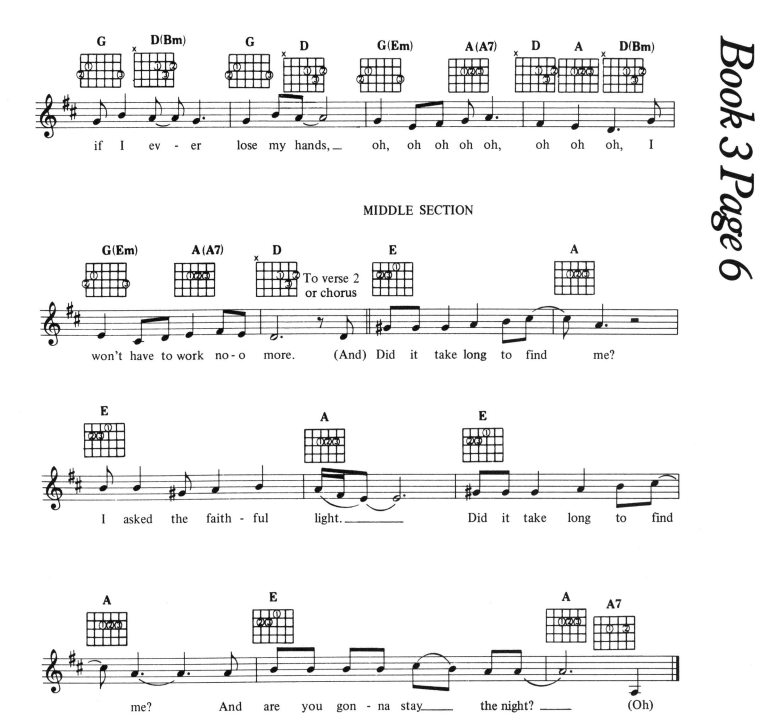

if I ev - er lose my hands, — oh, oh oh oh oh, oh oh oh, I

MIDDLE SECTION

won't have to work no - o more. (And) Did it take long to find me?

I asked the faith - ful light. _____ Did it take long to find

me? And are you gon - na stay ____ the night? _____ (Oh)

Note: Chords in brackets are possible substitutes for chords shown.

Verse 2:
And if I ever lose my eyes,
If my colour all runs dry,
Yes if I ever lose my eyes,
Oh , oh, oh, oh, oh, oh, oh, oh,
I won't have to cry no more.

Verse 3:
And if I ever lose my legs,
I won't moan and I won't beg
Oh if I ever lose my legs,
Oh, oh, oh, oh, oh, oh, oh, oh,
I won't have to walk no more.

Verse 4:
And if I ever lose my mouth,
All my teeth, North and South,
Yes if I ever lose my mouth,
Oh, oh, oh, oh, oh, oh, oh, oh,
I won't have to talk *(instrumental till end of next bar)*

Middle Section:
Did it take long to find me?
I asked the faithful light.
Did it take long to find me?
And are you gonna stay the night?
(Finish with chorus and repeat of last line of chorus.)

21

Jamaica Farewell Traditional, arranged Russ Shipton

4/4 Rhythm/Syncopated Calypso Rhythm/Strumming

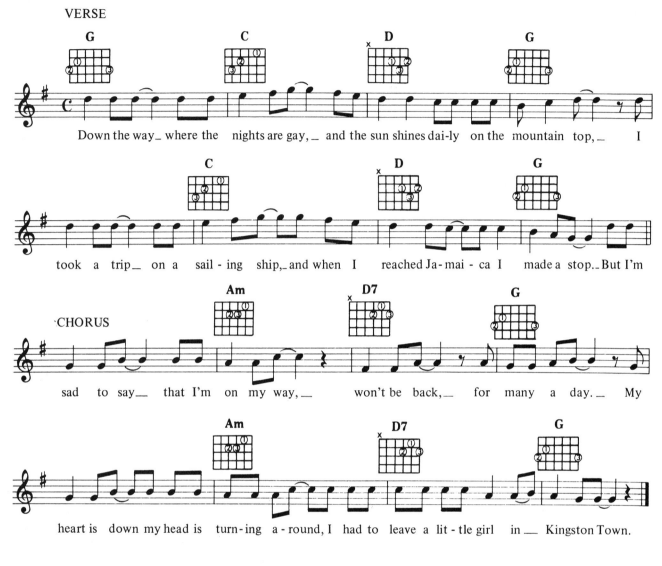

VERSE

G **C** **D** **G**

Down the way_ where the nights are gay,_ and the sun shines dai-ly on the mountain top,_ I

C **D** **G**

took a trip_ on a sail-ing ship,_ and when I reached Ja-mai-ca I made a stop._ But I'm

CHORUS

Am **D7** **G**

sad to say_ that I'm on my way,_ won't be back,_ for many a day._ My

Am **D7** **G**

heart is down my head is turn-ing a-round, I had to leave a lit-tle girl in_ Kingston Town.

Verse 2:
Down in the market you can hear
Ladies cry out as on their heads they bear
Akkai rice, salt fish are nice
And the rum is fine any time of year.

Verse 3:
Sounds of laughter everywhere
And the dancing girls swing to and fro'.
I must declare my heart is there
Though I've been from Maine to Mexico.

Michael Row The Boat Ashore Traditional, arranged Russ Shipton

4/4 Rhythm/Swing Strum Pattern

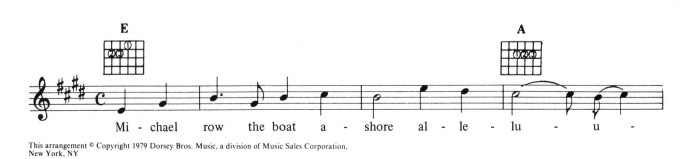

E **A**

Mi-chael row the boat a-shore al-le-lu-u-

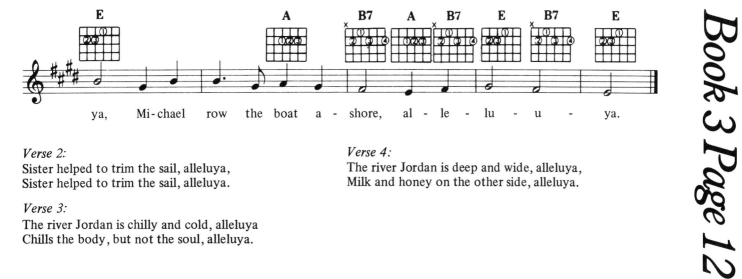

ya, Mi-chael row the boat a - shore, al - le - lu - u - ya.

Verse 2:
Sister helped to trim the sail, alleluya,
Sister helped to trim the sail, alleluya.

Verse 3:
The river Jordan is chilly and cold, alleluya
Chills the body, but not the soul, alleluya.

Verse 4:
The river Jordan is deep and wide, alleluya,
Milk and honey on the other side, alleluya.

Morning Has Broken Cat Stevens

3/4 Rhythm/Bass-Strum/Mixed Patterns with Runs and Hammer-ons

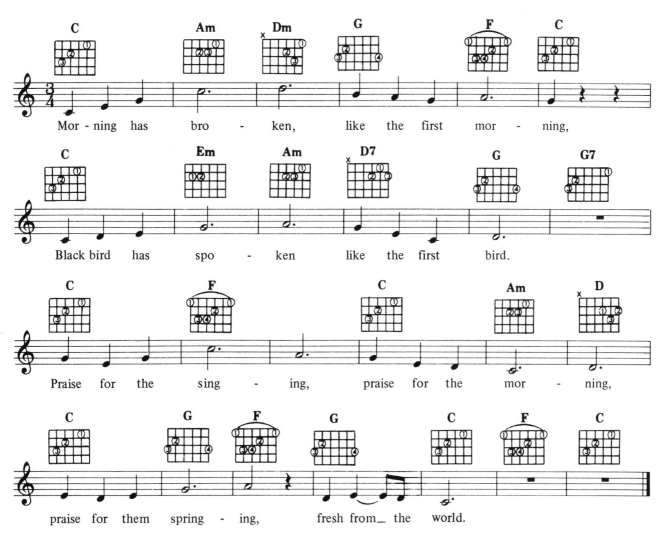

Mor - ning has bro - ken, like the first mor - ning,

Black bird has spo - ken like the first bird.

Praise for the sing - ing, praise for the mor - ning,

praise for them spring - ing, fresh from the world.

Verse 2:
Sweet the rain's new fall, sunlit from heaven,
Like the first dew fall on the first grass,
Praise for the sweetness of the wet garden
Sprung in completeness, where his feet pass.

Verse 3:
Mine is the sunlight, mine is the morning
Born of the one light Eden saw play.
Praise with elation, praise every morning
God's recreation of the new day.

She'll Be Coming Round The Mountain

Traditional, arranged Russ Shipton

4/4 Rhythm/Bass-Strum/Mixed Patterns/Melody Picking

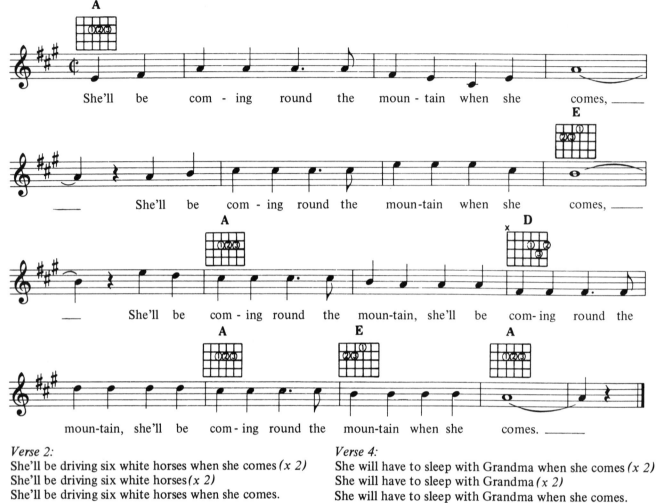

She'll be com - ing round the moun - tain when she comes, ___

___ She'll be com - ing round the moun-tain when she comes, ___

___ She'll be com - ing round the moun-tain, she'll be com - ing round the

moun-tain, she'll be com - ing round the moun-tain when she comes. ___

Verse 2:
She'll be driving six white horses when she comes *(x 2)*
She'll be driving six white horses *(x 2)*
She'll be driving six white horses when she comes.

Verse 3:
She'll be wearing pink pyjamas when she comes *(x 2)*
She'll be wearing pink pyjamas *(x 2)*
She'll be wearing pink pyjamas when she comes.

Verse 4:
She will have to sleep with Grandma when she comes *(x 2)*
She will have to sleep with Grandma *(x 2)*
She will have to sleep with Grandma when she comes.

Verse 5:
And we'll all go to meet her when she comes *(x 2)*
And we'll all go to meet her *(x 2)*
Oh we'll all go to meet her when she comes.

Goin' Places Russ Shipton

4/4 Rhythm/Swing Arpeggio Patterns/Instrumental

1st Section

2nd Section   (Not in Student's Book)

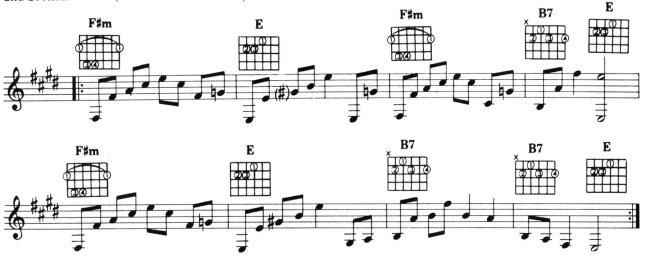

[Note: Read all first notes of quaver couplets as dotted, and second notes as semiquavers, as shown in the first bar]

Where Have All The Flowers Gone? Traditional, arranged Russ Shipton

4/4 Rhythm/Arpeggio Pattern with Runs and Pinches

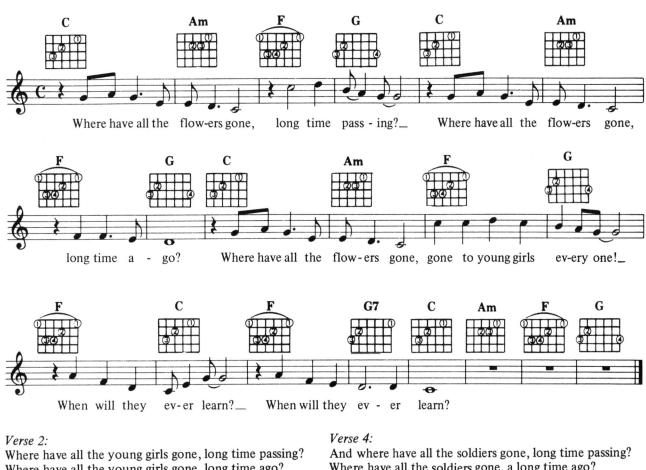

Where have all the flow-ers gone, long time pass-ing?_ Where have all the flow-ers gone,

long time a - go? Where have all the flow-ers gone, gone to young girls ev-ery one!_

When will they ev-er learn?_ When will they ev - er learn?

Verse 2:
Where have all the young girls gone, long time passing?
Where have all the young girls gone, long time ago?
Where have all the young girls gone?
Gone to young men everyone!
When will they ever learn, when will they ever learn?

Verse 3:
Where have all the young men gone, long time passing?
Where have all the young men gone, long time ago?
Where have all the young men gone?
Gone to soldiers, every one!
When will they ever learn, when will they ever learn?

Verse 4:
And where have all the soldiers gone, long time passing?
Where have all the soldiers gone, a long time ago?
Where have all the soldiers gone?
Gone to graveyards, every one!
When will they ever learn, when will they ever learn?

Verse 5:
And where have all the graveyards gone, long time passing?
Where have all the graveyards gone, long time ago?
Where have all the graveyards gone?
Gone to flowers, every one!
When will they ever learn, when will they ever learn?

Suzanne Leonard Cohen

4/4 Rhythm/Syncopated Arpeggio Pattern

26

Verse 2:
And Jesus was a sailor
When he walked upon the water
And he spent a long time watching
From his lonely wooden tower,
And when he knew for certain
Only drowning men could see him
He said "All men will be sailors then
Until the sea shall free them."
But he himself was broken
Long before the sky would open
Foresaken almost human,
He sank beneath your wisdom like a stone.

Verse 3:
Now Suzanne takes your hand
And she leads you to the river
She is wearing rags and feathers
From Salvation Army counters.
And the sun pours down like honey
On our lady of the harbour;
And she shows you where to look
Among the garbage and the flowers.
There are heroes in the seaweed,
There are children in the morning,
They are leaning out for love
And they will lean that way forever,
While Suzanne holds the mirror.

This Train   Traditional, arranged Russ Shipton

4/4 Rhythm/Alternating Thumb/Mixed Patterns

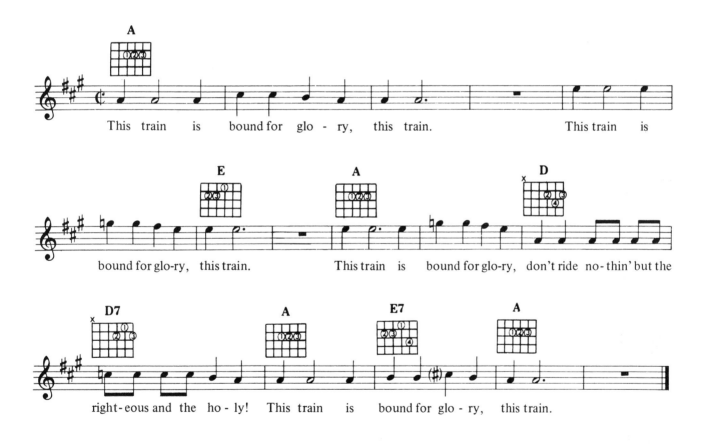

Verse 2:
This train don't carry no gamblers, this train *(x 2)*
This train don't carry no gamblers
No midnight ramblers, no bar fliers!
This train is bound for glory, this train.

Verse 3:
This train don't carry no liars, this train *(x 2)*
This train don't carry no liars
No hypocrites and no bar fliers!
This train is bound for glory, this train.

Verse 4:
This train don't carry white or black, this train *(x 2)*
This train don't carry white or black,
Everybody's treated all alike!
This train is bound for glory, this train.

Streets Of London   Ralph McTell

4/4 Rhythm/Alternating Thumb/Mixed Patterns/Embellishments and Pinches

VERSE

Have you seen the old man in the closed down mar-ket, pick - ing up the pa-per, with his worn out shoes? In his eyes you see no pride and held loose-ly by his side, yes-ter-day's pa-pers, tell-in' yes-ter-day's news. So how can you tell me you're lo - one - ly, and say for you that the sun don't shine?

CHORUS

Let me take you by the hand and lead you through the streets of Lon - don, I'll show you some-thing, to make you change your mind.

Verse 2:
Have you seen the old gal who walks the streets of London,
Dirt in her hair and her clothes in rags?
She's no time for talking, she just keeps right on walking
Carrying her home in two carrier bags.

Verse 3:
And in the all-night café, at a quarter past eleven
Some old man sitting there on his own
Looking at the world over the rim of his tea-cup
Each tea lasts an hour, then he wanders home alone.

Verse 4:
And have you seen the old man outside the Seaman's mission
His memory's fading with those medal ribbons that he wears
And in our winter city, the rain cries a little pity
For one more forgotten hero, and a world that doesn't care.

Take Me Home Country Roads

Bill Danoff, Taffy Nivert, and John Denver

4/4 Rhythm/Alternating Thumb/More Mixed Patterns/Embellishments and Pinches/ Instrumental Introduction

VERSE

Al-most hea-ven, West Vir - gin - ia the Blue Ridge Mountains, the She-nan-do-ah

ri - ver. Life is old there, old-er than the trees, young-er than the mountains,

CHORUS

blow -in' like a breeze. Country roads, take me home, to the place

where I be - long, West Vir - gin-ia, mountain momma, take me

MIDDLE SECTION (Not in Student's Book)

home, country roads. I hear her voice, in the mor-ning, how she calls me, the

ra - di - o re - minds me of my home far a - way. Driv-in' down the road I get a

(to chorus)

feel - in' that I should be home, yes-ter - day, yes-ter - day. (Country)

Verse 2:
All my memories gather round her a river's lady and a stranger to blue water,
Dark and dusty, painted on the sky, the misty taste of moonshine on the teardrop in my eye.

Study Fernando Carulli

"Bass-Pluck" Classical Piece

Section 1

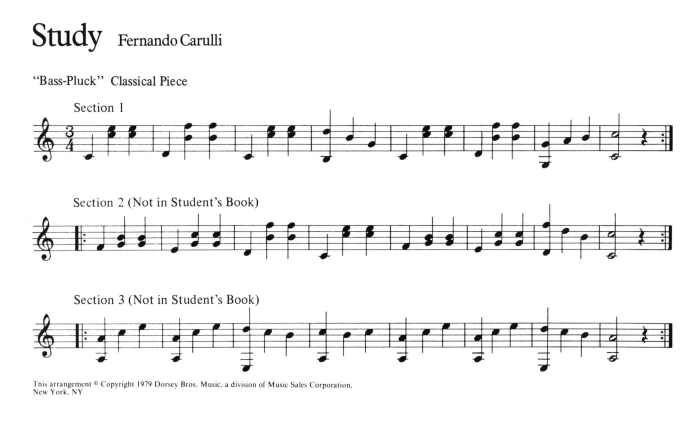

Section 2 (Not in Student's Book)

Section 3 (Not in Student's Book)

Passing Note Waltz Russ Shipton

Classical Style/Passing Notes

Section 1

Section 2 (Not in Student's Book)

Call And Answer Russ Shipton

2/4 Rhythm/Switching from Bass to Treble lines

Section 1

Section 2 (Not in Student's Book)

(strum)

And I Love Her Lennon/McCartney

4/4 Rhythm/Strumming with barré shapes

VERSE

I give her all my love, that's all I

do, ___ and if you saw my love, you'd love her too, ___ and I

MIDDLE SECTION

do. ___ A love like ours, will ne - ver

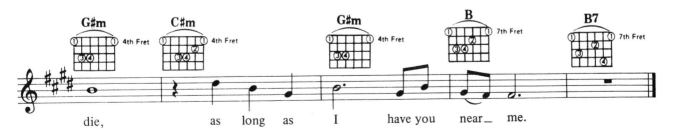

die, as long as I have you near _ me.

Verse 2:
She gives me everything, and tenderly
The kiss my lover brings, she brings to me
And I love her.

Verse 3:
Bright are the stars that shine, dark is the sky
I know this love of mine will never die
And I love her.

Mellow Yellow Donovan

4/4 Swing Rhythm/Damping

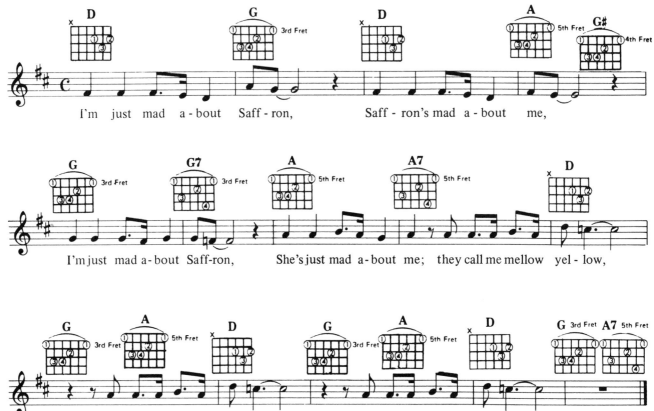

I'm just mad a-bout Saff-ron,   Saff-ron's mad a-bout   me,

I'm just mad a-bout Saff-ron,   She's just mad a-bout me; they call me mellow   yel - low,

they call me mellow   yel - low,   they call me mellow   yel - low.   Oh yeah!

Verse 2:
I'm just mad about fourteen, fourteen's mad about me,
I'm just mad about fourteen, fourteen's mad about me.
They call me mellow yellow, they call me mellow yellow,
They call me mellow yellow.

Verse 3:
Born high forever to fly, wind velocity nil
Born high forever to fly, if you want your cup I will fill.
They call me mellow yellow, they call me mellow yellow,
They call me mellow yellow.

Verse 4:
Electrical banana, is gonna be a sudden craze,
Electrical banana, is bound to be the very next phase.
They call me mellow yellow, they call me mellow yellow,
They call me mellow yellow.

Freight Train James and Williams

4/4 Rhythm/Alternative Thumb/Picking the Melody

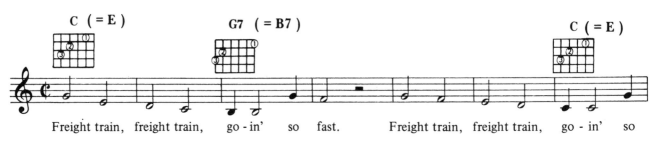

Freight train, freight train,   go - in'   so   fast.   Freight train, freight train, go - in' so

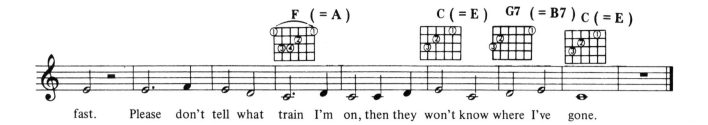

fast.   Please   don't   tell   what   train   I'm   on,   then   they   won't   know   where   I've   gone.

Verse 2:
When I'm dead and in my grave
No more good times will I crave.
Place the stones at my head and feet
And tell them that I've gone to sleep.

Verse 4:
When I die Lord bury me deep
Way down on old Chestnut Street,
Place the stones at my head and feet
And tell them that I'm still asleep.

Verse 3:
When I die Lord bury me deep
Way down on old Chestnut Street
So I can hear old number nine
As she comes rollin' by.

Note: Put your capo on the 4th fret (the C, F and G7 chord shapes that you then finger
will actually be the E, A and B7 chords).

Sunday Blues Russ Shipton

4/4 Rhythm/Monotonic Bass style/Hammer-ons on to the beat

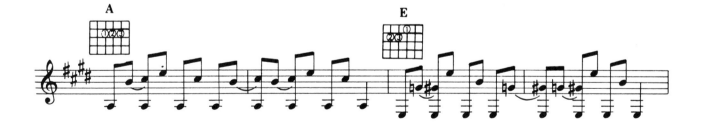

Down By The Brook   Russ Shipton

4/4 Rhythm/Alternating Thumb/Pull-offs

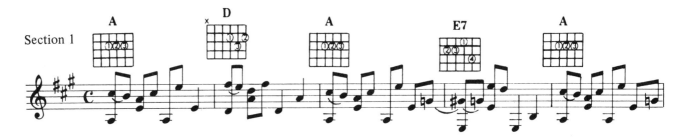

Section 1

Section 2 (Not in Student's Book)

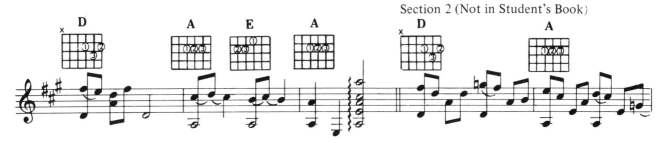

(to Section 1)

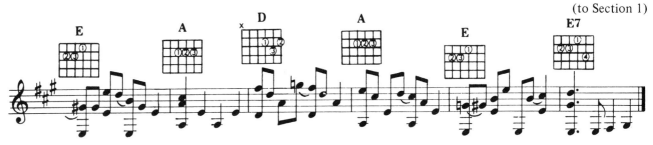

Skateboarding In The Park   Russ Shipton

3/4 Rhythm/Slides   (Note: Full chords are not desired in all cases)

Section 1

Section 2 (Not in Student's Book)

(to Start)

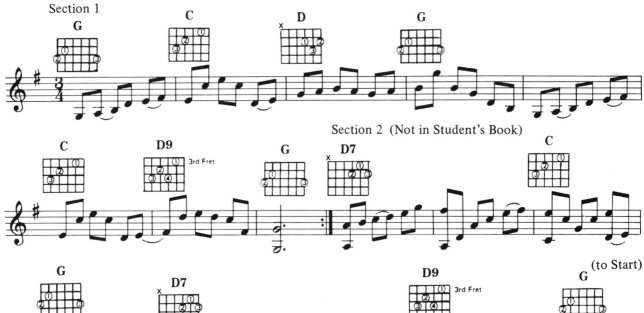

34

Little Ben (Clock Chime) Russ Shipton

Harmonics [◆ = harmonic]

Watermelon Russ Shipton

4/4 Rhythm/D Bass Tuning

(Low E string tuned down to D)

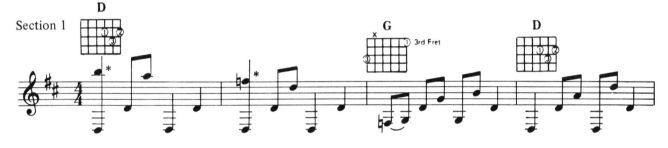

Section 2

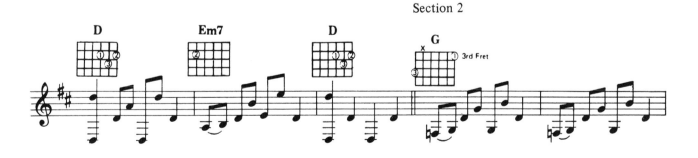

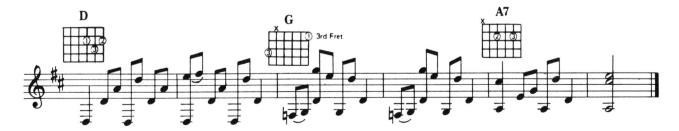

* = bend this note slightly sharper

If You Could Read My Mind   Gordon Lightfoot

4/4 Rhythm/Mixed Styles and Patterns

If   you could   read   my   mind   love,   what a   tale   my

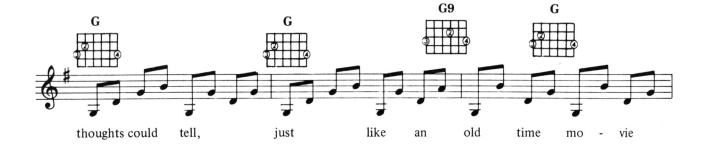

thoughts could   tell,   just   like   an   old   time   mo - vie

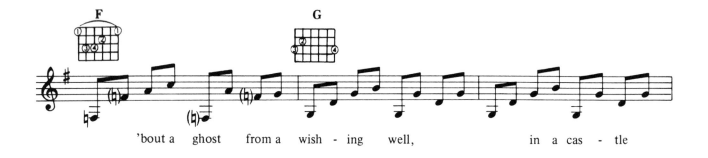

'bout a   ghost   from a   wish - ing   well,   in a   cas - tle

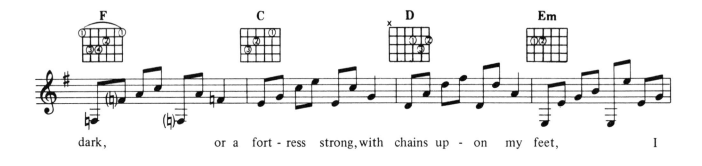

dark,   or a   fort - ress   strong, with   chains   up - on   my   feet,   I

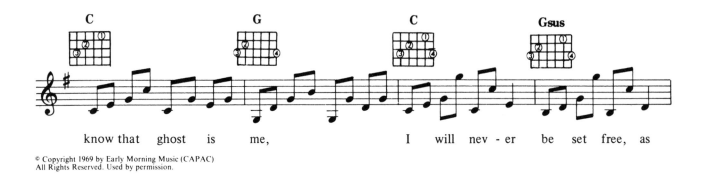

know that   ghost   is   me,   I   will   nev - er   be   set   free,   as

36

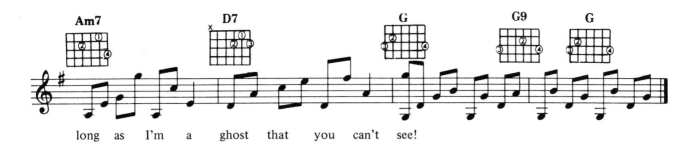

long   as   I'm   a   ghost   that   you   can't   see!

Verse 2:

If I could read your mind love, what a tale your thoughts could tell
Just like a paperback novel, the kind that drug stores sell.
Then you reached the part where the heartaches come, the hero would be me,
But heroes often fail, and you won't read that book again
Because the ending's just too hard to take!

Middle Section (Not in Student's Book):
```
G        G(add9)   C              D           Em
I'd walk away, like a movie star who gets burned in a three-way script,
  C       G     C        G            Am        D        Em
Enter number two: a movie queen to play the scene of bringing all the good things out of me.
        C          G     C             G
But for now love, let's be real — I never thought I could feel this way
      Am        D         C            G
And I've got to say that I just don't get it. I don't know where we went wrong,
      Am           D        G     G(add9)
But the feeling's gone and I just can't get it back!
```

Verse 3:

If you could read my mind love, what a tale my thoughts could tell,
Just like an old time movie, 'bout a ghost from a wishing well,
In a castle dark, or a fortress strong, with chains upon my feet,
But stories always end, and if you read between the lines
You'd know that I'm just trying to understand the feelings that you lack.
I never thought I could feel this way and I've got to say that I just don't get it,
I don't know where we went wrong, but the feeling's gone and I just can't get it back!

Air In C   Fernando Sor

The classical "Pinch and" style

Greensleeves Traditional, arranged Russ Shipton

3/8 Rhythm/Classical Style

Section 1

Section 2 (Not in Student's Book)

Study Fernando Sor

Holding Notes/Embellishments in the Classical Style

Section 1

Section 2

Study Continued

Section 3

Study Carcassi

4/4 Rhythm/Study Semiquavers

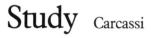

Dance Traditional, arranged Russ Shipton

6/8 Rhythm/Classical Style

Section 1

Section 2

Romanza Traditional, arranged Russ Shipton

Quaver Triplets in the Classical Style.

(Note: Each group of 3 quavers is equal to 2 quavers)   i.e.

The Complete Guitar Player Songbook No. 2

by Russ Shipton

Amsco Publications
London/New York/Sydney/Cologne

Amsco Publications
New York/London/Sydney

Music Sales Corporation
225 Park Avenue South, New York, NY 10003 USA

Music Sales Limited
8/9 Frith Street, London W1V 5TZ England

Music Sales Pty. Limited
120 Rothschild Street, Rosebery, Sydney, NSW 2018, Australia

This book Copyright © 1982 by Wise Publications.
Published 1984 by Amsco Publications,
A Division of Music Sales Corporation, New York, NY.

International Standard Book Number: 0.8256.2328.6

Art direction by Mike Bell

Printed in the United States of America by
Vicks Lithograph and Printing Corporation

Tablature sample (one bar)

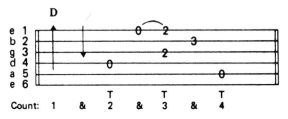

Notes:

a) D (indicated above tab.) = chord to be fingered.

b) ↑ = *down*ward strum.

c) ↓ = *up*ward strum.

d) Numbers on lines (strings) = open string or fret to be fingered and played.

e) 0⌢2 = an open string hammered on to the 2nd fret.

f) T (indicated below tab.) = right hand thumb. For other notes, right hand fingers are used.

g) Where 'swing' is indicated before the song, the notes between beats are delayed.

America   Paul Simon

Book 1

3/4 Rhythm/Strumming.
See Course Book No. 1 Page 9.

"Kathy," I said, as we boarded a Greyhound in Pittsburgh
"Michigan seems like a dream to me now.
"It took me four days to hitchhike from Saginaw
"I've come to look for America."
Laughing on the bus, playing games with the faces
She said the man in the gaberdine suit was a spy
I said "Be careful, his bowtie is really a camera
Toss me a cigarette, I think there's one in my raincoat."
"We smoked the last one an hour ago."
So I looked at the scenery, she read her magazine
And the moon rose over an open field
"Kathy, I'm lost," I said, though I knew she was sleeping
"I'm empty and aching and I don't know why."
Counting the cars on the New Jersey Turnpike
They've all come to look for America
All come to look for America
All come to look for America.

Bill Bailey   Traditional, arranged Russ Shipton

4/4 Rhythm/Strumming.
See Course Book No. 1 Page 12.

"Won't you come home, Bill Bai-ley, won't you come home?" She moans the whole day long.____

"I'll do the cook-ing, darl-ing, I'll pay the rent, I know I've done you wrong.____ Re-

-mem-ber that rain-y eve-ning, I drove you out, with no-thing but a fine tooth comb? __ I

know I'm to blame, well ain't that a shame? Bill Bai-ley, won't you please come home?"__

Whiskey In The Jar   Traditional, arranged Russ Shipton

4/4 Rhythm/Strumming/Lively.
See Course Book No. 1 Page 12.

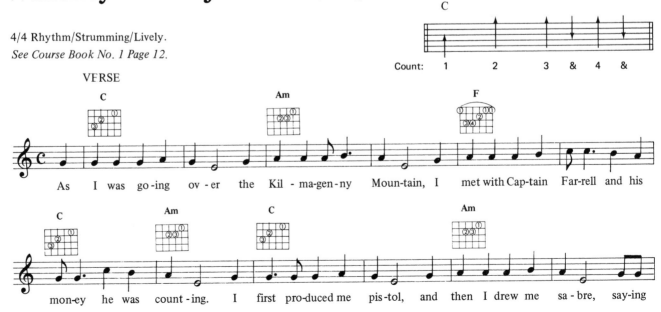

VERSE

As I was go-ing ov-er the Kil-ma-gen-ny Moun-tain, I met with Cap-tain Far-rell and his

mon-ey he was count-ing. I first pro-duced me pis-tol, and then I drew me sa-bre, say-ing

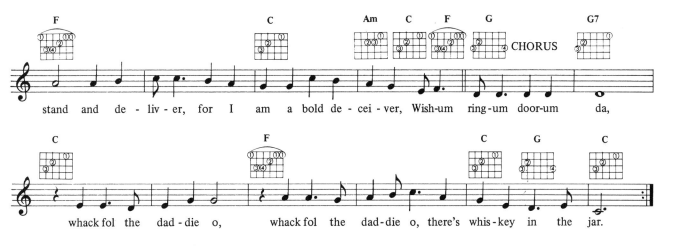

stand and de - liv - er, for I am a bold de - cei - ver, Wish-um ring-um door-um da, whack fol the dad - die o, whack fol the dad - die o, there's whis-key in the jar.

Verse 2:
He counted out his money, and it made a pretty penny
I put it in me pocket, and took it home to Jenny
She sighed and she swore that she never would betray me
But the devil take the women for they never can be easy.

Verse 3:
I went into me chamber, for to take a slumber
I dreamt of gold and jewels and for sure it was no wonder
For Jenny drew me charges, and she filled them up with water
And she sent for Captain Farrell to be ready for the slaughter.

Verse 4:
And it was early in the morning, before I rose to travel
Up comes a band of footmen and likewise Captain Farrell
I then produced me pistol, for she'd stole away me sabre
But I couldn't shoot the water, so a prisoner I was taken.

Verse 5:
Now if anyone can aid me, it's me brother in the army
If I could learn his station be it Cork or in Killarney
And if he'd come and join me, we'd go roving in Kilkenny
I'll engage he'd treat me fairer than me darling sporting Jenny.

Guantanamera Words by Jose Marti. Music adaptation by Hector Angulo & Pete Seeger

4/4 Rhythm/Strumming.
See Course Book No. 1 Page 14.

Count: 1 2 & 3 & 4 &

CHORUS

Guan-taname-ra, gua-ji-ra Guanta-name-ra, Guanta-name - ra, gua-ji-ra Guan-ta-na-me - - ra.

VERSE

Yo soy un hombre sincero, De donde cre-ce la pal-ma. Yo soy un hombre since - ro, De donde cre - ce la pal-ma. Y antes de mo-rir-me quie - ro, E-char mis versos del al - ma.

Verse 2:
Mi verso es de un verde claro
Y de un carmin encendido
Mi verso es un cierro herido
Que busca en el monte amparo.

Verse 3:
Con los pobres de la tierra
Quiero yo mi suerte echar
El arroyo de la sierra
Me complace mas que el mar.

The Wreck Of The Edmund Fitzgerald Gordon Lightfoot

3/4 Rhythm/Strumming.
See Course Book No. 1 Page 14.

Aadd9

Count: 1   2 & 3 &

1. The leg-end lives on from the Chip-pe-wa on down, of the big lake they call "Git-che   Gu-mee."
2. The lake, it   is said, nev-er   gives up her dead, when the skies of No-vem-ber turn   gloom-y.
3. With a load of iron ore twenty six thou-sand tons more than the Ed-mund Fitz-ge-rald weighed emp-ty,
4. That good ship and true was a   bone to be chewed, when the gales of No-vem-ber came   ear-ly.

Verse 2:

The ship was the pride of the American side
Coming back from some mill in Wisconsin.
As the big freighters go it was bigger than most
With a crew and good captain well-seasoned.
Concluding some terms with a couple of steel firms
When they left fully loaded for Cleveland.
And later that night when the ship's bell rang
Could it be the north wind they'd been feeling?

Verse 3:

The wind in the wires made a tattletale sound
And a wave broke over the railing
And every man knew as the captain did too
'Twas the witch of November come stealing.
The dawn came late and the breakfast had to wait
When the gales of November came slashing.
When afternoon came it was freezing rain
In the face of a hurricane west wind.

Verse 4:

When suppertime came the old cook came on deck saying:
"Fellas, it's too rough to feed you."
At seven p.m. a main hatchway caved in, he said:
"Fellas, it's been good to know you."
The captain wired in he had water coming in
And the good ship and crew was in peril.
And later that night when his lights went out of sight
Came the wreck of the Edmund Fitzgerald.

Verse 5:

Does anyone know where the love of God goes
When the waves turn the minutes to hours?
The searchers all say they'd have made Whitefish Bay
If they'd put fifteen more miles behind her.
They might have split up or they might have capsized
They may have broke deep and took water.
And all that remains is the faces and the names
Of the wives and the sons and the daughters.

Verse 6:

Lake Huron rolls, Superior swings in
In the rooms of her ice-water mansion.
Old Michigan steams like a young man's dreams
The island and bays are for sportsmen.
And farther below Lake Ontario
Takes in what Lake Erie can send her.
And the iron boats go as the mariners all know
With the gales of November remembered.

Verse 7:

In a musty old hall in Detroit they prayed
In the Maritime Sailors' Cathedral.
The church bell chimed till it rang twenty nine times
For each man on the Edmund Fitzgerald.
The legend lives on from the Chippewa on
Down of the big lake they called Gitche Gumee.
"Superior", they said, "never gives up her dead"
"When the gales of November come early."

6

Wild World Cat Stevens

4/4 Rhythm/Ballad strum.

See Course Book No. 1 Page 14.

Count: 1 2 3 & 4 &

VERSE

Now that I've lost eve-ry-thing to you,— you said you want to start some-thing new, and it's break-in' my heart you

leav - ing, ba-by I'm grievin'. But if you wan-na leave, take good care, hope you have a lot of nice things to

CHORUS

wear,— but then a lot of nice things turn bad___ out there. Oh

ba - by, ba – by, it's a wild world, it's hard to get by, just u-pon a smile. Oh

ba - by, ba – by, it's a wild world, I'll al - ways re - member you just like a child, girl.

Verse 2:
You know I've seen a lot of what the world can do
And it's breaking my heart in two
Because I never want to see you sad, girl
Don't be a bad girl
But if you wanna leave, take good care
Hope you make a lot of nice friends out there
But just remember there's a lot of bad air and beware.

Homeward Bound   Paul Simon

4/4 Rhythm/Bass-strum.
See Course Book No. 1 Pages 14 & 22.

Verse 2:

Every day's an endless stream
Of cigarettes and magazines
And each town looks the same to me
The movies and the factories
And every stranger's face I see
Reminds me that I long to be.

Verse 3:

Tonight I'll sing my songs again
I'll play the game and pretend
But all my words come back to me
In shades of mediocrity
Like emptiness in harmony
I need someone to comfort me.

The Universal Soldier Buffy Sainte-Marie

4/4 Rhythm/Bass - strum.

See Course Book No. 1 Page 15.

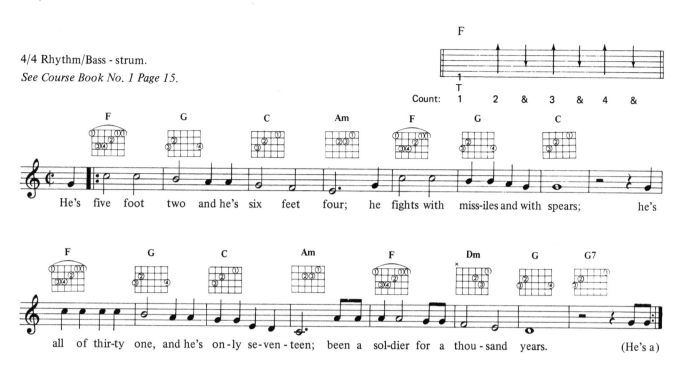

He's five foot two and he's six feet four; he fights with miss-iles and with spears; he's

all of thir-ty one, and he's on-ly se-ven-teen; been a sol-dier for a thou-sand years. (He's a)

Verse 2:
He's a Catholic, a Hindu, an Atheist, a Jain
A Buddhist and a Baptist and a Jew
And he knows he shouldn't kill, and he knows he always will
Kill you for me, my friend, and me for you.

Verse 3:
And he's fighting for Canada, he's fighting for France
He's fighting for the U.S.A.
And he's fighting for the Russians and he's fighting for Japan
And he thinks we'll put an end to war this way.

Verse 4:
And he's fighting for democracy, he's fighting for the Reds
He says it's for the peace of all
He's the one who must decide who's to live and who's to die
And he never sees the writing on the wall.

Verse 5:
But without him how would Hitler have condemned him at Dachau?
Without him Caesar would have stood alone
He's the one who gives his body as a weapon of the war
And without him all this killing can't go on.

Verse 6:
He's the universal soldier, and he really is to blame
His orders come from far away no more
They come from here and there, and you and me
And Brothers, can't you see
This is not the way we put an end to war.

Sweet Baby James James Taylor

3/4 Rhythm/Bass - strum.

See Course Book No. 1 Page 17.

VERSE

There is a young cow-boy he lives on the range, _____ his horse and his cat - tle are his

on - ly com - pan - ions. _____ He works in the sad-dle and he sleeps in the can-yons, wait-ing for sum-mer, his

past -ures to change. _____ And as the moon ri - ses he sits by his fire,

think-in' 'bout wo - men and glass-es of beer. and clos-ing his eyes as the dog-gies re - tire, he sings out a

song which is soft but it's clear, as if may- be some-one could hear.

CHORUS

Good-night you moon-light lad - ies, rock-a-bye sweet ba - by James, deep greens and blues are the

col -ours I choose, won't you let me go down in my dreams, and rock- a - bye sweet ba - by James.

Verse 2:
Now the first of December was covered in snow
And so was the turnpike from Stockbridge to Boston
The Berkshires seemed dreamlike on account of that frosting
With ten miles behind me and ten thousand more to go
There's a song that they sing when they take to the highway
A song that they sing when they take to the sea
A song that they sing of their home in the sky
Maybe you can believe it if it helps you to sleep
But singing works just fine for me.

The Waltz Of Love   Russ Shipton

3/4 Rhythm/Bass - strum.
See Course Book No. 1 Page 22.

VERSE

There is a dance hall that seems to be free, where blind men come bold-ly, so sure they can see, the

band plays "It's ea-sy like one two three." Let's dance to the waltz— of love.

CHORUS

Come waltz with me, dance to life's sweet-est sound. I'll lead you first till you twist me ar - ound,

fast- er in cir - cles then fall to the ground. Let's dance to the waltz— of love.

Verse 2:
Out on the dance floor we smile and we stare
Our feet move with someone who cannot be there
While the band plays the old and familiar air
Let's dance to the waltz of love.

Verse 3:
Down off the clouds maybe crawl from the floor
Some fools protest yet they come back for more
They hear the band play "Love is life, so be sure —
You dance to the waltz of love".

The Wild Rover

Book 1

Traditional, arranged Russ Shipton

3/4 Rhythm/Bass - strum/Lively.
See Course Book No. 1 Page 22.

VERSE

I've been a wild ro-ver for ma-ny a year,___ and I've spent all me mon-ey on whis-key and beer.___ But now I'm re-turn-ing with gold in great store,___ and I ne-ver will play the wild ro-ver no more; and it's no, nay nev-er,___ no nay nev-er, no more,___ will I play___ the wild ro-ver,___ no nev-er,___ no more.___

CHORUS

Verse 2:
I went to an alehouse I used to frequent
And I told the landlady me money was spent
I asked her for credit, she answered me "Nay"
"Such custom as yours I could have any day".

Verse 3:
I took out of me pocket ten sovereigns bright
And the landlady's eyes opened wide with delight
She said "I have whiskeys and wines of the best
And the words that you told me were only in jest."

Verse 4:
I'll go home to me parents, confess what I've done
And ask them to pardon their prodigal son
And when they've caressed me as oftimes before
I never will play the wild rover no more.

12

Both Sides Now   Joni Mitchell

4/4 Rhythm/Simple arpeggio with moving bass line.
See Course Book No. 1 Page 27.

Verse 2:
Moons and Junes, and Ferris wheels
The dizzy, dancing way you feel
As every fairy tale comes real
I've looked at love that way.
But now it's just another show
You leave 'em laughing when you go
And if you care, don't let them know
Don't give yourself away.
I've looked at love from both sides now
From give and take and still somehow
It's love's illusions I recall
I really don't know love at all.

Verse 3:
Tears and fears and feeling proud
To say "I love you" right out loud
Dreams and schemes and circus crowds
I've looked at life that way.
But now old friends are acting strange
They shake their heads, they say I've changed
But something's lost and something's gained
In living every day.
I've looked at life from both sides now
From win and lose and still somehow
It's life's illusions I recall
I really don't know life at all.

Slip Slidin' Away   Paul Simon

4/4 Rhythm/Strumming/Swing/Stress 2nd and 4th beats.
See Course Book No. 2 Page 5.

CHORUS

Slip slid - in' a-way,   slip slid - in' a - way,_____   you know the near-er your des-tin-a-tion, the

more you're slip slid - in' a way.   I know a man,___   he came from my home town.

He wore his pass-ion for his wo-man like a thor-ny crown.   He said "De-lor - es, ___   I   live in

fear.___   My love for you is so over-pow'ring I'm a - fraid that I   will dis - app - ear.

Verse 2:
I know a woman
Became a wife
These are the very words she uses to describe her life
She said "A good day ain't got no rain"
She said "A bad day is when I lie in bed"
"And think of things that might have been."

Verse 3:
And I know a father
Who had a son
He longed to tell him all the reasons for the things he'd done
He came a long way just to explain
He kissed the boy as he lay sleeping
Then he turned around and headed home again.

Verse 4:
God only knows
God makes his plan
The information is unavailable to the mortal man
We work our jobs, collect our pay
Believe we are gliding down the highway
When in fact we are slip slidin' away.

San Francisco Bay Blues   Jesse Fuller

4/4 Rhythm/Strumming/Swing/Lively.
Book 2 Page 8.

VERSE 1

I got the blues when my ba-by left me by the San-Francis - co   Bay.   She's taken an oc-ean lin - er and she's

14

Lyin' Eyes   Don Henley and Glenn Frey

4/4 Rhythm/Strumming.
See Course Book No. 2 Page 10.

Verse 2:
Late at night a big old house gets lonely
I guess every form of refuge has its price
And it breaks her heart to think her love is only
Given to a man with hands as cold as ice.

Verse 3:
So she tells him she must go out for the evening
To comfort an old friend who's feeling down
But he know's where she's going as she's leaving
She is headed for the cheating side of town.

Verse 4:
On the other side of town a boy is waiting
With fiery eyes and dreams no-one could steal
She drives on through the night anticipating
'Cause he makes her feel the way she used to feel.

Verse 5:
She rushes to his arms, they fall together
She whispers that it's only for a while
She swears that soon she'll be coming back forever
She pulls away and leaves him with a smile.

Verse 6:
She gets up and pours herself a strong one
And stares out at the stars up in the sky
Another night, it's gonna be a long one
She draws the shade and hangs her head to cry.

Verse 7:
She wonders how it ever got this crazy
She thinks about a boy she knew in school
Did she get tired or did she just get lazy
She's so far gone she feels just like a fool.

Verse 8:
My, oh my, you sure know how to arrange things
You set it up so well, so carefully
Ain't it funny how your new life didn't change things
You're still the same old girl you used to be.

Money's The Word

Russ Shipton

4/4 Rhythm/Strumming/Stress 2nd upstroke.
See Course Book No. 2 Page 10.

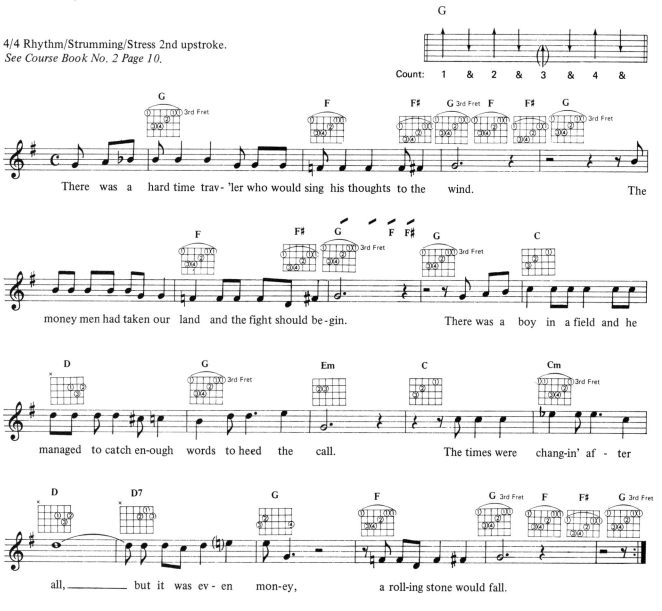

There was a hard time trav- 'ler who would sing his thoughts to the wind. The

money men had taken our land and the fight should be-gin. There was a boy in a field and he

managed to catch en-ough words to heed the call. The times were chang-in' af-ter

all, _____ but it was ev-en mon-ey, a roll-ing stone would fall.

Verse 2:
Now the magic man has long since gone to ground
For the music is lost in his soul and can't be found
And since the tambourine man's tambourine, up and turned to rust
The waiting list it waits, and eyes the prince's purse . . . .
But it's even money — there's a prophet's curse.

Verse 3:
There's a man from the west and he's playin' real cool guitar
And there's a guy from the east who's followin' a northern star
There's a guy underground writing longer words in lines that don't even rhyme
And the one on the inside who claims he's seen a sign . . . .
But it's even money — they've all hit the wrong time.

Verse 4:
Well the hard time traveller must be cryin' where he lays
And-a-wondrin' just what he was fighting for all his days
For the sun went down on the time when songs were sung like the call of a bird
The music man plugged in, sold out, as the businessman he stirred . . . .
And it's even money — money's the word,
Money's the word, money's the word, money's the word.

Sundown   Gordon Lightfoot

4/4 Rhythm/Strumming/Stress 2nd and 4th beats.
See Course Book No. 2 Page 10.

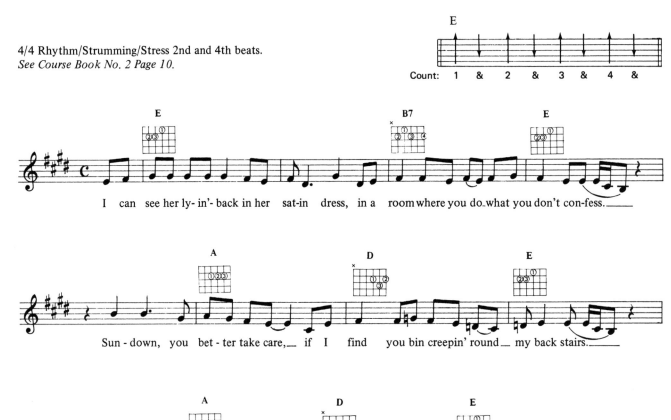

I can see her ly-in'-back in her sat-in dress, in a room where you do what you don't con-fess.

Sun-down, you bet-ter take care,— if I find you bin creepin' round — my back stairs.

Sun-down, you bet-ter take care,— if I find you bin creepin' round my back stairs.—

Verse 2:
She's been lookin' like a queen in a sailor's dream
And she don't always say what she really means
Sometimes I think it's a shame
When I get feelin' better when I'm feelin' no pain
Sometimes I think it's a shame
When I get feelin' better when I'm feelin' no pain.

Verse 3:
I can picture every move that a man could make
Gettin' lost in her lovin' is your first mistake
Sundown, you better take care
If I find you bin creepin' round my back stairs
Sometimes I think it's a shame
When I get feelin' better when I'm feelin' no pain.

Verse 4:
I can see her lookin' fast in her faded jeans
She's a hard lovin' woman got me feelin' mean
Sometimes I think it's a shame
When I get feelin' better when I'm feelin' no pain
Sundown, you better take care
If I find you bin creepin' round my back stairs.

Take It Easy

Jackson Browne & Glenn Frey

4/4 Rhythm/Strumming/Stress 2nd and 4th beats.
See Course Book No. 2 Page 10.

Verse 2:
Well I'm a-standin' on a corner in Winslow, Arizona
And such a fine sight to see
It's a girl, my Lord, in a flat bed Ford
Slowin' down to take a look at me
Come on baby, don't say maybe
I gotta know if your sweet love is gonna save me
We may lose and we may win
Though we will never be here again
So open up, I'm climbin' in
So take it easy.

Verse 3:
Well I'm a-runnin' down the road tryin' to loosen my load
I gotta world of trouble on my mind
Lookin' for a lover who won't blow my cover
She's so hard to find
Take it easy, take it easy
Don't let the sound of your own wheels make you crazy
Come on baby, don't say maybe
I gotta know if your sweet love is gonna save me.

The Black Velvet Band
Traditional, arranged Russ Shipton

6/8 Rhythm/Bass-strum.

See Course Book No. 2 Page 12.

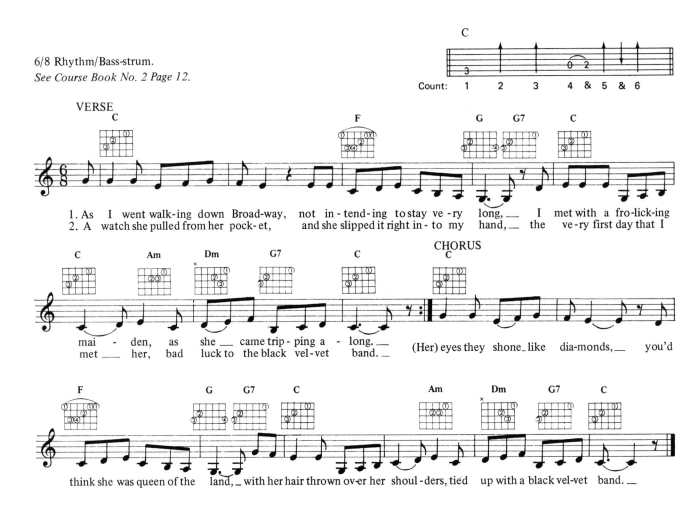

VERSE

1. As I went walk-ing down Broad-way, not in-tend-ing to stay ve-ry long, __ I met with a fro-lick-ing
2. A watch she pulled from her pock-et, and she slipped it right in-to my hand, __ the ve-ry first day that I

mai - den, as she __ came trip-ping a - long. __
met __ her, bad luck to the black vel-vet band. __

CHORUS

(Her) eyes they shone __ like dia-monds, __ you'd think she was queen of the land, __ with her hair thrown ov-er her shoul-ders, tied up with a black vel-vet band. __

Verse 2:
'Twas in the town of Tralee
An apprenticeship to trade I was bound
With plenty of bright amusement
To see the days go round.
Till misfortune and trouble came over me
Which caused me to stray from my land
Far away from me friends and relations
To follow the black velvet band.

Verse 3:
Before the judge and the jury
The both of us had to appear
And a gentleman swore to the jewellery —
the case against us was clear.
For seven years' transportation
Right over to Van Dieman's land
Far away from me friends and relations
To follow the black velvet band.

Verse 4:
Come all you brave, young Irish lads
A warning take by me
Beware of all the pretty young damsels
That are knocking around in Tralee.
They'll treat you to whisky and porter
Until you're unable to stand
And before you have time for to leave them
You're bound for Van Dieman's land.

Ridin' Blind Russ Shipton

4/4 Rhythm/Bass - strum/Steady.
See Course Book No. 2 Page 15.

Count: 1 2 & 3 & 4 &

VERSE

With the peo-ple _____ who aren't an-y - where, watch-in' all the clouds form from light - er air. The ave-rage man, like a knife, _ falls through here the out-skirts of

CHORUS

life. _____ Am - ster-dam, _ where _ are you? So far a - head, _ yet still be - hind; _____ a thou-sand steps from no-where, still look-ing for a sign, _____ smile u-pon us lost souls rid - in' blind. _____

Verse 2:
Seats for 50, holding 15
An American clinger and a loose-tongued singer, if you know what I mean
Roller coasters, too many toasters
A madman keeping the stage from the queen.

Verse 3:
Sufi Castenada Buddha, kindred spirits roam
Wander thru these precious grounds, saved from sea and foam
Here the searchin' wanderers come
With too much time to lose and space to run.

Imagine John Lennon

4/4 Rhythm/Arpeggio.
See Course Book No. 2 Page 20.

VERSE

I - ma-gine there's no hea - ven, it's ea - sy if you try,

no hell be - low us, a - bove us on - ly sky. I - ma-gine all the

peo - ple liv - ing for to - day, a - ha. You may say ___ I'm a

MIDDLE SECTION

dream-er but I'm not the on - ly one. I hope some day ___ you'll

join us, and the world ___ will live as one. ___

Verse 2:
Imagine there's no countries
It isn't hard to do
Nothing to kill or die for
And no religion too.
Imagine all the people
Living life in peace, aha.

Verse 3:
Imagine no possessions
I wonder if you can
No need for greed or hunger
A brotherhood of man.
Imagine all the people
Sharing all the world, aha.

Kumbaya Traditional, arranged Russ Shipton

4/4 Rhythm/Arpeggio.
See Course Book No. 2 Page 20.

Verse 2:
Someone's crying Lord, Kumbaya
Someone's crying, Lord, Kumbaya
Someone's crying, Lord, Kumbaya
Oh Lord, Kumbaya.

Verse 3:
Someone's praying, Lord, Kumbaya
Someone's praying, Lord, Kumbaya
Someone's praying, Lord, Kumbaya
Oh Lord, Kumbaya.

Verse 4:
Someone's singing, Lord, Kumbaya
Someone's singing, Lord, Kumbaya
Someone's singing, Lord, Kumbaya
Oh Lord, Kumbaya.

April Come She Will Paul Simon

4/4 Rhythm/Alternating thumb.
See Course Book No. 2 Page 23.

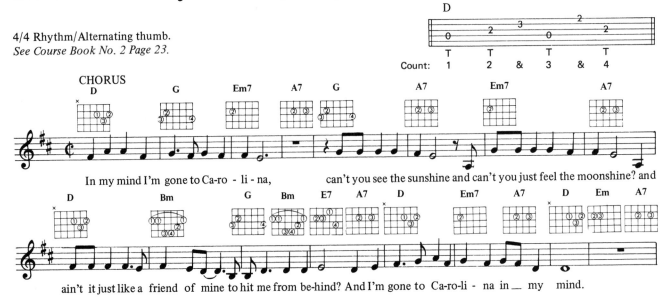

A - pril. Come she will, When streams are ripe and swelled with rain. May _____ she will stay, _____ rest-ing in my arms a - gain.

A love once new has now grown __ old.

Verse 2:
June, she'll change her tune
In restless walks she'll prowl the night
July, she will fly
And give no warning to her flight.

Verse 3:
August, die she must
The autumn winds blow chilly and cold
September, I'll remember
A love once new, has now grown old.

Carolina In My Mind James Taylor

4/4 Rhythm/Alternating thumb.
See Course Book No. 2 Page 23.

CHORUS

In my mind I'm gone to Ca-ro - li - na, can't you see the sunshine and can't you just feel the moonshine? and

ain't it just like a friend of mine to hit me from be-hind? And I'm gone to Ca-ro-li - na in __ my mind.

Kar-in she's a silver sun you'd best walk her away and watch it shine. Watch her watch the morning come.

sil - ver tear ap-pearing now, I'm cry - ing, ain't I? I'm gone to Ca - ro - li - na in_ my mind.

LAST SECTION

Now with a hol - y host of oth-ers stand-ing round_ me, Still I'm on the dark side of_ the moon,

To Chorus

and it seems like it goes on like this for ev-er, you must for - give_____ me.

Verse 2:

Dark and silent, late last night
I think I might have heard the highway call
Geese in flight and dogs that bite
And signs that might be omens say I'm going, going
I'm gone to Carolina in my mind.

Verse 3:

There ain't no doubt in no-one's mind
That love's the finest thing around
Whisper something soft and kind
And hey, babe, the sky's on fire, I'm dying, ain't I?
I'm gone to Carolina in my mind.

The Sloop John B. Traditional, arranged Russ Shipton

4/4 Rhythm/Alternating thumb.
See Course Book No. 2 Page 23.

VERSE/CHORUS

We come on the Sloop John B., my grand pap-py and me. Round Nass-au Town we_ did roam,

drink-in' all night, got in-to a fight, oh I feel so broke up I wan-na go home.

Chorus:

So hoist up the John B. sails
See how the mains'ls set
Send for the captain ashore
Let me go home, let me go home
Let me go home, I feel so broke-up
I wanna go home.

Verse 2:

The first mate, he got drunk
Broke up the people's trunk
Constable had to come and take him away
Sheriff Johnstone, please let me alone
I feel so broke-up
I wanna go home.

Only Hopes Returning   Russ Shipton

4/4 Rhythm/Alternating thumb.
See Course Book No. 2 Page 25.

Verse 2:
I'm like a flower trying to bloom in Winter snows
I'm like the North wind wondrin' where to blow
I see your smiling face,
I miss every line and trace
And in my dreams you call me sweet and low.

Verse 3:
I'm trapped just like the convict in his cell
Goin' over and over those things I knew so well
I'd love to hear the sound
Of your footsteps on the ground
You know I'd reach the door before you touched the bell.

Help John Lennon and Paul McCartney

4/4 Rhythm/Strumming/Fast.
See Course Book No. 3 Page 6.

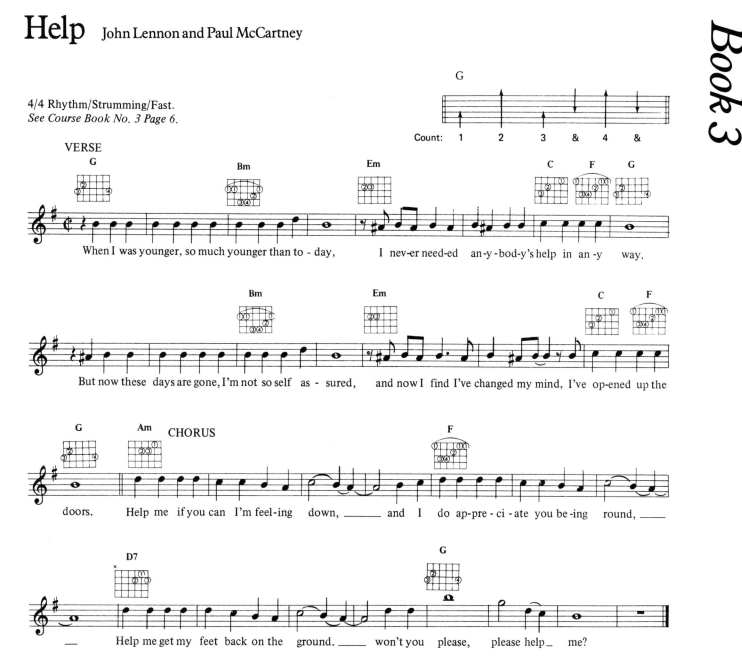

Verse 2:
And now my life has changed in oh so many ways.
My independence seems to vanish in the haze.
But every now and then I feel so insecure
I know that I just need you like I've never done before.

Frankie And Johnny   Traditional, arranged Russ Shipton

4/4 Rhythm/Bass-strum/Swing.
See Course Book No. 3 Page 11.

Fran-kie and John-ny were lov-ers, ___ oh lord-y how they could love. They swore to be true to each oth-er true as the stars a - bove. He was her man, but he was do-ing her wrong.

Verse 2:
Frankie, she was a good woman
As everybody knows
Spent a hundred dollars
Just to buy her man some clothes
He was her man, but he was doing her wrong.

Verse 3:
Frankie went down to the corner
Just for a bucket of beer
She said "Oh Mister bartender"
"Has my loving Johnny been here?"
He was her man, but he was doing her wrong.

Verse 4:
"Now I don't wanna tell you no stories
And I don't wanna tell you no lies
I saw Johnny 'bout an hour ago
With a gal named Nelly Bligh."
He was her man, but he was doing her wrong.

Verse 5:
Now Frankie went down to the hotel
Didn't go there for fun
Underneath her long dress
She carried a forty-four gun
He was her man, but he was doing her wrong.

Verse 6:
Well the first time that Frankie shot Johnny
He let out an awful yell
Second time that she shot him
There was a new man's face in hell.
He was her man, but he was doing her wrong.

Worried Man Blues   Traditional, arranged Russ Shipton

4/4 Rhythm/Bass - strum/Slight swing.
See Course Book No. 3 Page 11.

CHORUS/VERSE

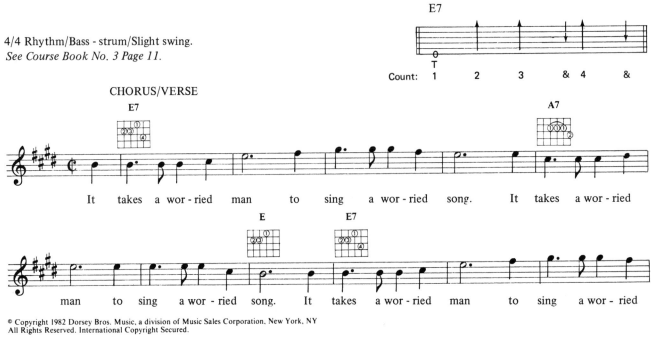

It takes a wor-ried man to sing a wor-ried song. It takes a wor-ried man to sing a wor-ried song. It takes a wor-ried man to sing a wor-ried

song, I'm wor - ried now, _____ but I won't be wor - ried long. _____

Verse 2:
I went across the river, and I lay down to sleep
I went across the river, and I lay down to sleep
I went across the river, and I lay down to sleep
When I woke up, I had shackles on my feet.

Verse 3:
When everything goes wrong, I sing a worried song
When everything goes wrong, I sing a worried song
When everything goes wrong, I sing a worried song
I'm worried now, but I won't be worried long.

All My Trials   Traditional, arranged Russ Shipton

4/4 Rhythm/Syncopated arpeggio.
See Course Book No. 3 Page 16.

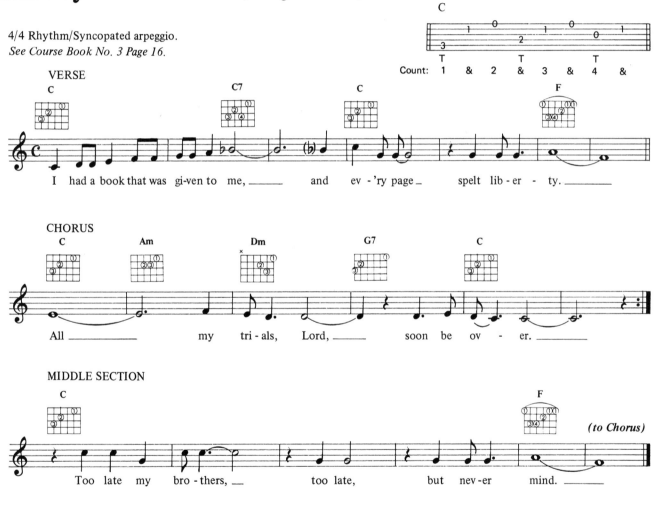

VERSE

I had a book that was gi-ven to me, _____ and ev -'ry page _ spelt lib - er - ty. _____

CHORUS

All _____ my tri - als, Lord, _____ soon be ov - er. _____

MIDDLE SECTION

Too late my bro - thers, _ too late, but nev -er mind. _____ *(to Chorus)*

Verse 2:
If religion were a thing that money could buy
The rich would live, and the poor would die.

Verse 3:
There is a tree in paradise
The pilgrims call it the tree of life.

Verse 4:
Jordan water is chilly and cold
Chills the body, but not the soul.

Verse 5:
Hush little baby, don't you cry
Your momma was born to die.

Book 3

Diamonds And Rust Joan Baez

4/4 Rhythm/Syncopated arpeggio.
See Course Book No. 3 Page 16.

VERSE

1. Well, I'll be damned, here comes your ghost a - gain, but that's not un - us - u - al,
2. And here I sit, hand on the tel - e - phone, I'm hear - ing a voice I'd known

it's just that the moon is full, and you happ -ened to call.
a cou - ple of light years ago, head - ing straight for a fall.

MIDDLE SECTION

Now I see you stand - ing with brown leaves fall - ing all a - round and snow in your hair. Now you're

smil - ing out the win-dow of that crum-my ho-tel ov - er Wash-ing-ton Square. Our breath comes out white clouds,

mingles and hangs in the air. Speak-ing strict-ly for me, we both could have died then and there.

Verse 2:
As I remember
Your eyes were bluer than robins' eggs
My poetry was lousy, you said
Where are you calling from?
A booth in mid-west.
Ten years ago
I bought you some cufflinks
You bought me something
We both know what memories can bring
They bring diamonds and rust.

Verse 3:
You burst on the scene
Already a legend
The unwashed phenomenon
The original vagabond
You strayed into my arms.
And there you stayed
Temporarily lost at sea
The madonna was yours for free
Yes the girl on the half shell
Could keep you unharmed.

Verse 4:
Now you're telling me you're not nostalgic
Then give me another word for it
You who're so good with words
And at keeping things vague.
'Cause I need some of that vagueness now
It's all come back too clearly
Yes I loved you dearly
And if you're offering me diamonds and rust
I've already paid.

30

Your Song
Elton John & Bernie Taupin

4/4 Rhythm/Syncopated arpeggio with pinches.
See Course Book No. 3 Page 16.

VERSE

It's a lit-tle bit fun-ny,___ this feel-ing in - side,___ I'm not one of those who can eas-i-ly

hide, ___ don't have much mon-ey, but___ boy if I did,___ I'd buy a big house where ___

CHORUS (from Vs. 2 and 4)

we both could live. you. And you can tell eve-ry-bo-dy this is your

song.___ It may be quite sim-ple but now that it's done, ___ I hope you don't mind_ I hope you don't mind

that I put down in words, how won-der-ful life is while you're_ in the world.___

Verse 2:
If I was a sculptor, but then again, no
Or a man who makes potions in a travelling show
I know it's not much but, it's the best I can do
My gift is my song, and this one's for you.

Verse 3:
I sat on the roof, and kicked off the moss
Well a few of the verses, they got me quite cross
But the sun's been quite kind while I wrote this song
It's for people like you that keep me turned on.

Verse 4:
So excuse me forgetting, but these things I do
You see I've forgotten if they're green or they're blue
Anyway, the thing is, what I really mean
Yours are the sweetest eyes I've ever seen.

Mr Bojangles
Jerry Jeff Walker

3/4 Rhythm/Arpeggio/Swing.
See Course Book No. 3 Page 17.

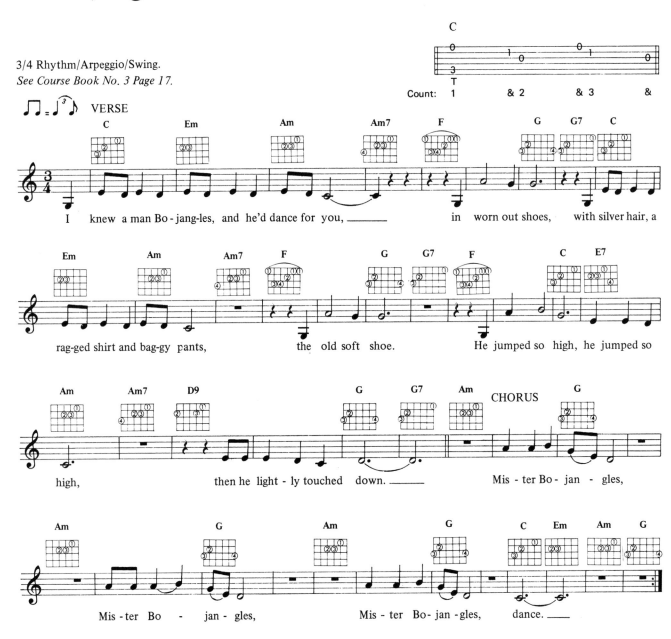

VERSE

I knew a man Bo-jang-les, and he'd dance for you, _____ in worn out shoes, with silver hair, a

rag-ged shirt and bag-gy pants, the old soft shoe. He jumped so high, he jumped so

high, then he light-ly touched down. _____ CHORUS Mis-ter Bo-jan-gles,

Mis-ter Bo - jan-gles, Mis-ter Bo-jan-gles, dance. _____

Verse 2:
I met him in a cell in New Orleans I was, down and out
He looked at me to be the eyes of age, as he spoke right out
He talked of life, talked of life
He laughed, slapped his leg a step.

Verse 3:
He said his name, Bojangles, then he danced a lick across the cell
He grabbed his pants for a better stance then he jumped so high
He clicked his heels
Then he let go a laugh, let go a laugh
Shook back his clothes all around.

Verse 4:
He danced for those at minstrel shows and county fairs
Throughout the South
He spoke with tears of fifteen years how his dog and him
Travelled about
His dog up and died, he up and died
And after twenty years he still grieved.

Verse 5:
He said "I dance now at every chance in honky tonks
For drinks and tips
But most the time I spend behind these county bars
For I drinks a bit."
He shook his head, and as he shook his head
I heard someone ask "Please".

I'll Have To Say I Love You In A Song

Jim Croce

4/4 Rhythm/Syncopated arpeggio.
See Course Book No. 3 Page 20.

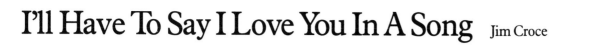

VERSE
Well I know it's kind-a late, I hope I did-n't wake you, but what I

got to say can't wait, I hope you'd un-der-stand.

CHORUS
Ev-ery time I tried to tell you the words just came out wrong, so I'll

have to say I love you in a song.

Verse 2:
Yeah I know it's kinda strange
But every time I'm near you
I just run out of things to say
I know you'd understand.

Verse 3:
Yeah I know it's kinda late
I hope I didn't wake you
But there's something that I just got to say
I know you'd understand.

Plumstones Russ Shipton

4/4 Rhythm/Syncopated arpeggio.

See Course Book No. 3 Page 20.

VERSE

A child of the twen-ties, that was my fath-er's time and all the dreams he might have had were fruit left up-on the

vine and ne-ver picked. He learnt a trick or two, the cavalry it saw him through. But that was a-no-ther day, when

CHORUS

nose to the grind-stone was the on-ly way. Tin-ker, tai-lor, sol-dier, sail-or, which one will you be?

Rich man, poor man, beggar man, thief,—lit-tle boy on my knee, don't let your dreams go free.

ENDING

see, but don't let your dreams go free._____

Verse 2:
A child of the fifties
Born with a new age dawning
I had bigger brighter better dreams
But in my head was my father's warning
Son, you've got to play the game
Work is still a sacred name
But that was another day
When freedom was just a word
We'd learnt to say.

Verse 3:
A child of the eighties
Here on my knee you sit
Counting all your plumstones
Just the way I did
When I was young
And you have your dreams too
All the things you'd like to do
It's not just another day
You can live your dreams
Don't throw 'em away.

Last Chorus:
Tinker, tailor, soldier, sailor
Which one will you be?
Rich man, poor man, beggarman, thief?
Little boy on my knee
Count your plumstones and see
But don't let your dreams go free.

34

There But For Fortune
Phil Ochs

Book 3

4/4 Rhythm/Syncopated arpeggio.
See Course Book No. 3 Page 20.

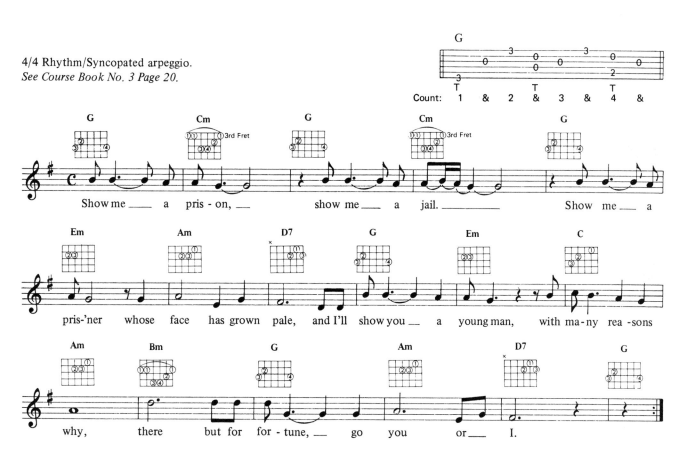

Show me ___ a pris-on, ___ show me ___ a jail. _____ Show me ___ a
pris-'ner whose face has grown pale, and I'll show you ___ a young man, with ma-ny rea-sons
why, there but for for-tune, ___ go you or ___ I.

Verse 2:
Show me an alley, show me a train
Show me a hobo who sleeps out in the rain
And I'll show you a young man with many reasons why
There but for fortune, go you or I.

Verse 3:
Show me the whiskey stains on the floor
Show me a drunk as he stumbles out the door
And I'll show you a young man with many reasons why
There but for fortune, go you or I.

Verse 4:
Show me a country where the bombs had to fall
Show me the ruins of buildings so tall
And I'll show you a young land with many reasons why
There but for fortune, go you or I.

The Boxer Paul Simon

4/4 Rhythm/Alternating thumb.
See Course Book No. 3 Page 23.

VERSE

I am just a poor boy, though my stor-y's sel-dom told, I have squand-ered my re-sis-tance for a pock-et-ful of mum-bles, such are pro-mi-ses. All lies and jest, still a man hears what he wants to hear, and dis-re-gards the rest, ooh la la, la la la la la la la.

CHORUS

Lie la lie, lie la lie la lie la lie, lie la lie, lie la lie la la la lie la la la la lie.

End of 4th verse

lead-ing me _____ go-ing home. _____

Verse 2:
When I left my home and my family, I was no more than a boy
In the company of strangers, in the quiet of a railway station
Running scared, laying low, seeking out the poorer quarters
Where the ragged people go, looking for the places only they
would know.

Verse 3:
Asking only workman's wages, I come looking for a job
But I get no offers, just a come-on from the whores on 7th
Avenue
I do declare, there were times when I was so lonesome
I took some comfort there.

Verse 4:
Then I'm laying out my winter clothes and wishing I was gone
Going home, where the New York City winters aren't bleeding
me

Leading me, going home.

Verse 5:
In the clearing stands a boxer, and a fighter by his trade
And he carries the reminders of every glove that laid him
down
Or cut him till he cried out in his anger and his shame
"I am leaving, I am leaving," but the fighter still remains.

36

Early Mornin' Rain Gordon Lightfoot

4/4 Rhythm/Alternating thumb.
See Course Book No. 3 Page 23.

Verse 2:

Out on runway number nine
Big seven-o-seven set to go
But I'm stuck here in the grass
Where the cold wind blows
Now the liquor tasted good
And the women all were fast
Well there she goes, my friend
She's rollin' now at last.

Verse 3:

Hear the mighty engines roar
See the silver bird on high
She's away and westward bound
Far above the clouds she'll fly
Where the mornin' rain don't fall
And the sun always shines
She'll be flyin' o'er my home
In about three hours time.

Verse 4:

This old airport's got me down
It's no earthly good to me
'Cause I'm stuck here on the ground
As cold and drunk as I can be
You can't jump a jet plane
Like you can a freight train
So I'd best be on my way
In the early mornin' rain.

Fire And Rain James Taylor

4/4 Rhythm/Arpeggio & alternating thumb mix.
See Course Book No. 3 Page 25.

VERSE

Just yes-ter-day morn-ing,_ they let me know you were gone, Su-san the plans they made put an

end to you. I walked out this morning, and I wrote down this song, I just can't re-

CHORUS

mem-ber who to send it to.__ I've seen fire and I've seen rain, I've seen

sun - ny days that I thought would never end, I've seen lonely times, when I could not find a

friend, but I always thought that I'd see you a - gain.

Verse 2:

Look down upon me Jesus, you gotta help me make a stand
You've just gotta see me through another day
My body's aching, and my time is at hand
And I won't make it any other way.

Verse 3:

Walking my mind to an easy time, my back turned towards the sun
Lord knows when the cold wind blows, it'll turn your head around
Well, those hours of time on the telephone line
To talk about things to come
Sweet dreams and flyin' machines in pieces on the ground.

Something George Harrison

4/4 Rhythm/Ballad strum.
See Course Book No. 4 Page 7.

Verse 2:
Somewhere in her smile, she knows
That I don't need no other lover
Something in her style that shows me
I don't want to leave her now
You know I believe and how.

Verse 3:
Something in the way she knows
And all I have to do is think of her
Something in the things she shows me
I don't want to leave her now
You know I believe and how.

Just The Way You Are Billy Joel

4/4 Rhythm/Strumming/Stress 1st beat and 1st upstroke slightly.
See Course Book No. 4 Page 10.

Verse 2:
Don't go trying some new fashion
Don't change the colour of your hair mm mm
You always have my unspoken passion
Although I might not seem to care.
I don't want clever conversation
I never want to work that hard, mm mm
I just want someone that I can talk to
I want you just the way you are.

Verse 3:
I said I love you, and that's forever
And this I promise from the heart, mm mm
I could not love you any better
I love you just the way you are.

40

May You Never
John Martyn

4/4 Rhythm/Slap style.
See Course Book No. 4 Page 11.

VERSE

May you ne - ver lay your head down___ with - out a hand to hold, may___ you

nev - er make your bed out in the cold___ You've been just like a good and close

sis-ter of mine, and you know I love you like I should. You nev-er talk a-bout me be - hind my back and I

CHORUS

know that there's times you could. Please won't you please won't you bear it in mind,___ love is a les - son to

learn in our time. Oh please, won't you please, won't you bear it in mind ___ for me.

Verse 2:
May you never lose your temper
If you get in a barroom fight
May you never lose your woman overnight.
You've been just like a good and close brother of mine
And you know I love you like I should.
You've got no knife to stab me in the back
And I know that there's those that would.

Sunny Afternoon
Raymond Douglas Davies

Book 4

4/4 Rhythm/Strumming/Swing/Damp downstrokes.
See Course Book No. 4 Page 11.

The tax-man's tak-en all my dough, and left me in my state-ly home,— laz - ing on a sun-ny aft - er -

noon. And I can't sail my yacht, he's tak-en ev'ry thing I've got.— All I've got's this sun - ny af-ter- noon.

Save me, save me, save me from this squeeze,— I've got a big fat mo-mma tryin' to break — me.

And I love to live so plea-sant-ly, live this life of lux - u-r - y, laz-ing on a sun-ny aft - er -

noon._____ in summer- time,___ in summer - time,___ in summer- time.___

Verse 2:
My girlfriend's gone off with my car
And gone back to her ma and pa
Telling tales of drunkenness and cruelty
Now I'm sitting here
Sipping at my ice-cold beer
Lazing on a sunny afternoon.
Help me, help me, help me sail away
You give me two good reasons
Why I ought to stay.
'Cause I love to live so pleasantly
Live this life of luxury
Lazing on a sunny afternoon
In summertime, in summertime, in summertime.

Here Comes The Sun George Harrison

4/4 Rhythm/Alternating thumb.
See Course Book No. 4 Page 14.

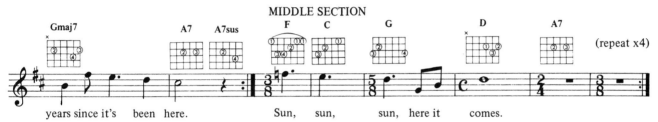

CHORUS

Here comes the sun.__ Here comes the sun.__ And I say "It's alright."

VERSE

Lit-tle darling, it's been a long, cold lone-ly win-ter. Lit-tle darling, it feels like

MIDDLE SECTION

(repeat x4)

years since it's been here. Sun, sun, sun, here it comes.

TAG (after last repeat of middle section)

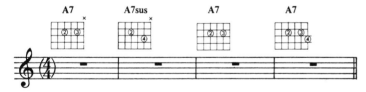

Verse 2:

Little darling, the smiles returning to their faces
Little darling, it seems like years since it's been here.

Verse 3:

Little darling, I feel that ice is slowly melting
Little darling, it seems like years since it's been clear.

Skyline Russ Shipton

3/4 Rhythm/Arpeggio and embellishments.
See Course Book No. 4 pages 16-22.

♩ = harmonic (always at 12th fret)

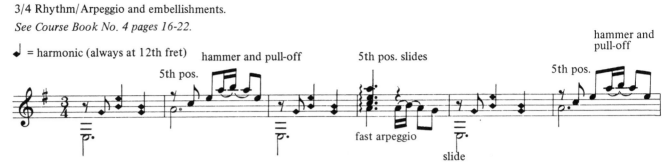

44

Snowmobiling Russ Shipton

4/4 Rhythm/Alternating thumb in D tuning with embellishments.
See Course Book No. 4 Pages 16-22.

1st   D
2nd   A
3rd   F#   'D' Tuning
4th   D
5th   A
6th   D

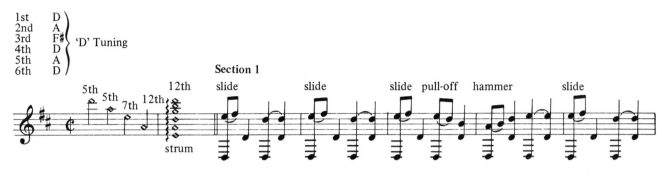

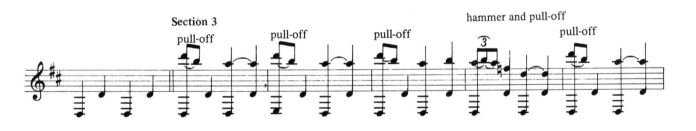

Book 4

The Third Waltz Russ Shipton

3/8 Rhythm/Arpeggio and embellishments with 3rds.
See Course Book No. 4 Pages 16-22 & 26.

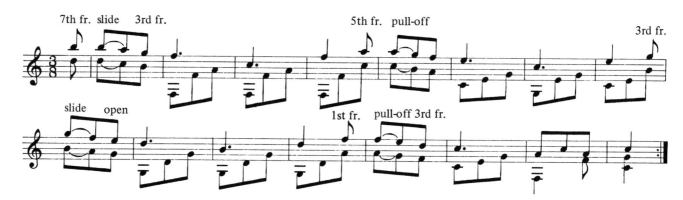

G.Wizz Russ Shipton

4/4 Rhythm/Syncopated arpeggio and alternating thumb mix. (Right hand thumb plays 1st & 2nd bass string notes in each bar,
See Course Book No. 4 Page 23.   one after the other).

Section 1

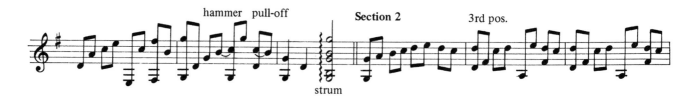

You've Got A Friend Carole King

4/4 Rhythm/Syncopated arpeggio and alternating thumb mix.
See Course Book No. 4 Page 23.

Verse 2:

If the sky, above you, should turn dark and full of clouds
And that old north wind should begin to blow
Keep your head together, and call my name out loud
And soon, you'll hear me knocking upon your door.

Book 4

Classical Capers Russ Shipton

6/8 Rhythm/Triplets and pinches.
See Course Book No. 4 Page 29.

Section 1

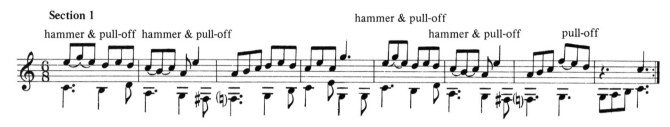

Section 2

Section 3

48

The Complete Guitar Player Songbook No.3

by Russ Shipton

Amsco Publications
New York/London/Sydney

Amsco Publications
New York/London/Sydney

Music Sales Corporation
225 Park Avenue South, New York, NY 10003 USA

Music Sales Limited
8/9 Frith Street, London W1V 5TZ England

Music Sales Pty. Limited
120 Rothschild Street, Rosebery, Sydney, NSW 2018, Australia

International Standard Book Number: 0.8256.2341.3

Art direction by Mike Bell

Printed in the United States of America by
Vicks Lithograph and Printing Corporation

Nights In White Satin   Justin Hayward

12/8 Rhythm (similar to 4 bars of 3/8)/Strumming
See Course Book No. 1 Page 7.

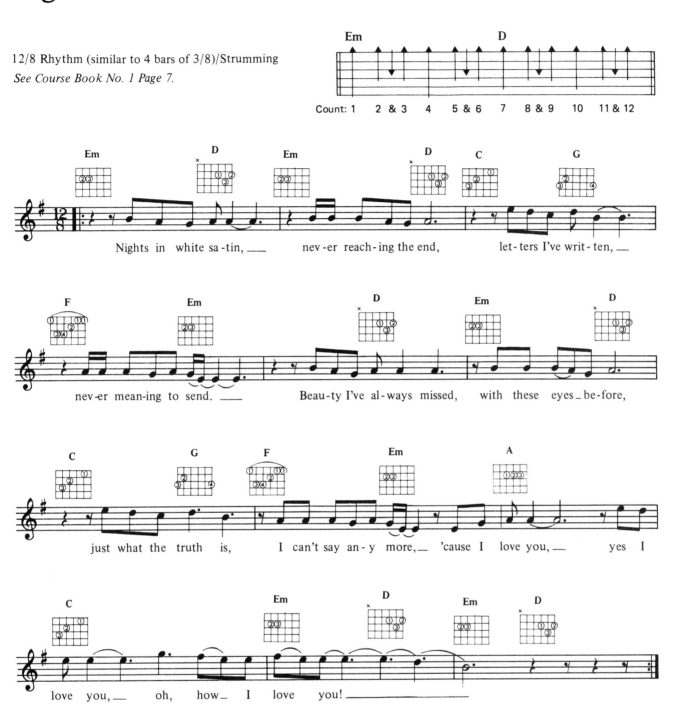

Nights in white sa-tin, ___ nev-er reach-ing the end, let-ters I've writ-ten, ___ nev-er mean-ing to send. ___ Beau-ty I've al-ways missed, with these eyes _ be-fore, just what the truth is, I can't say an-y more, __ 'cause I love you, __ yes I love you, __ oh, how _ I love you! _____

Verse 2
Gazing at people, some hand in hand
Just what I'm going through they can't understand
Some try to tell me thoughts they cannot defend
Just what you want to be, you'll be in the end
And I love you, yes I love you, Oh you I love you!

Help Me Make It Through The Night   Kris Kristofferson

4/4 Rhythm/Strumming

See Course Book No. 1 Page 12.

VERSE

Take the ribb-on from your hair, shake it loose and let it fall,

lay - in' soft up on my skin, like the shad-ows on the

wall. Help me make it through the night.

MIDDLE SECTION

I don't care what's right or wrong. I don't try to un-der - stand. _

Let the dev - il take to - mor-row, for to - night I need a friend.

Verse 2

Come and lay down by my side
Till the early mornin' light
All I'm takin' is your time
Help me make it through the night.

Verse 3

Yesterday is dead and gone
And tomorrow's out of sight
And it's sad to be alone
Help me make it through the night.

Mother And Child Reunion   Paul Simon

4/4 Rhythm/Strumming

See Course Book No. 1 Page 12.

CHORUS

No I would not give you false hope, on this strange and mourn-ful day,— but the mo-ther and child re - un-ion is on-ly a mo-ment a - way.—

VERSE

Oh, lit-tle dar-ling of mine, I can't for the life of me,— re-mem-ber a sad-der day. I know they say 'let it be',— but it just don't work out that way, and the course of a life-time runs ov-er and ov-er a - gain.—

Verse 2

Oh little darling of mine
I just can't believe it's so
And though it seems strange to say
I never bin laid so low
In such a mysterious way
And the course of a lifetime runs
Over and over again.

5

Sorry Seems To Be The Hardest Word

Elton John & Bernie Taupin

Book 1

Cut Time Rhythm (4/4 with extra stress on 1st & 3rd beats)/Strumming
See Course Book No. 1 Page 12.

Count: 1 2 3 & 4 &

VERSE

What have I got to do to make you love me? __ What have I got to do_ to make you

care? What do I do when light-ning strikes me, __ and I wake to find that you're not

there? What do I do to make you want me? __ What have I got to do _ to be

heard? What do I say when it's all ov-er? ___ Sor-ry seems to be the hard-est

MIDDLE SECTION

word. It's sad, __ it's so sad. __ It's a sad, sad sit - u - a - tion, __ and it's get-ting

more and more ab - surd. It's sad, __ it's so sad, __ why can't we talk it ov - er? __

Al - ways seems to me __ that sor - ry seems to be the hard-est word.

Bird On The Wire Leonard Cohen

3/4 Rhythm/Bass-strum

See Course Book No. 1 Page 15.

Verse 2

Like a worm, on a hook
Like a knight from some old-fashioned book
I have saved all my ribbons for thee.

Verse 3

Like a baby, stillborn
Like a beast with his horn
I have torn everyone who reached out for me.

Verse 4

So I swear by this song
I swear by all I did wrong
I will make it, I will make it, all up to you.

Middle Section 2

I saw a beggar leaning on his wooden crutch
He said to me "You must not ask for so much"
And a pretty woman leaning in her darkened door
She cried to me "Hey, why not ask for more?"

El Condor Pasa

English words Paul Simon
Musical arrangements J. Milchberg & D. Robles

4/4 Rhythm/Bass-pluck

See Course Book No. 1 Page 20.

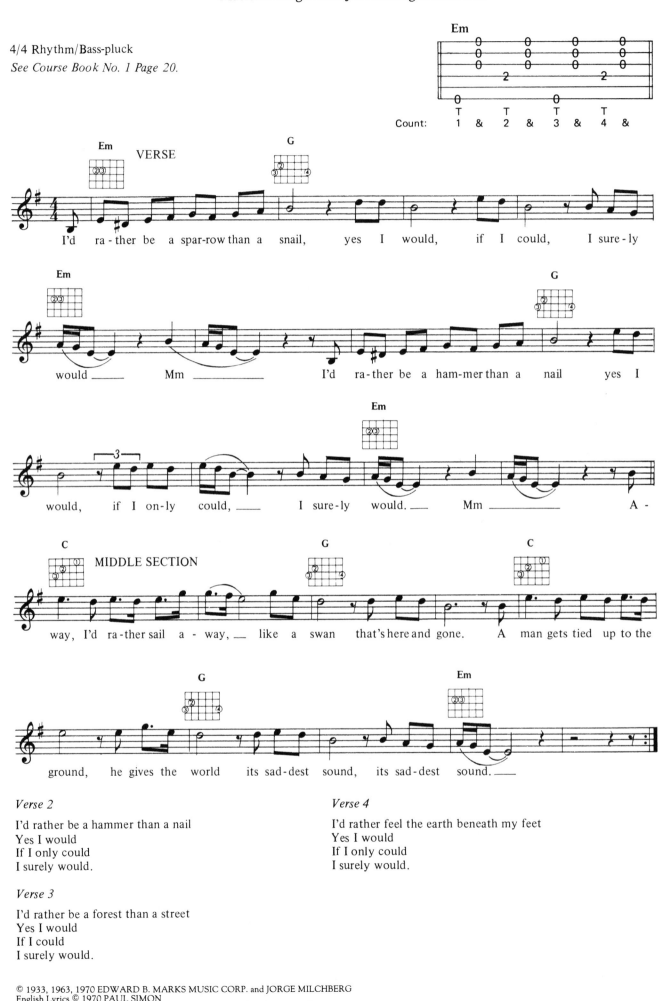

Verse 2

I'd rather be a hammer than a nail
Yes I would
If I only could
I surely would.

Verse 3

I'd rather be a forest than a street
Yes I would
If I could
I surely would.

Verse 4

I'd rather feel the earth beneath my feet
Yes I would
If I only could
I surely would.

Liverpool Lullaby

Words Stan Kelly
Music Traditional

Cut Time (4/4 with extra stress on 1st & 3rd beats)/Arpeggio
See Course Book No. 1 Page 25.

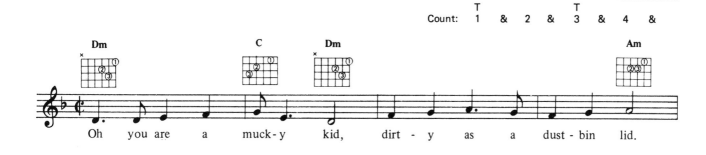

Oh you are a muck-y kid, dirt-y as a dust-bin lid.

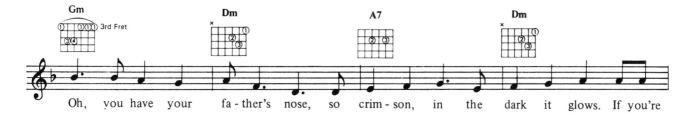

When he finds out the things you did, you'll get a belt from your dad.

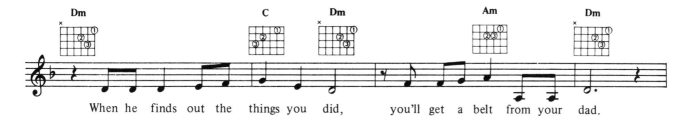

Oh, you have your fa-ther's nose, so crim-son, in the dark it glows. If you're

not a-sleep when the boo-zers close, you'll get a belt from your dad.

Verse 2

You look so scruffy lying there
Strawberry jam tufts in your hair
And in the world you haven't a care
And I have got so many
It's quite a struggle every day
Living on your father's pay
The bugger drinks it all away
Leaves me without any.

Verse 3

Although we have no silver spoon
Better days are coming soon
Now Nelly's working at the loom
And she gets paid on Friday
Perhaps one day we'll have a bath
When Littlewoods provides the cash
We'll get a house in Knotting Ash
And buy your Dad a brewery!

Verse 4

Oh you are a mucky kid
Dirty as a dustbin lid
When he finds out the things you did
You'll get a belt from your Dad
Oh you have your father's face
You're growing up a real hard case
But there's no-one else can take your place
Go fast asleep for mammy.

Turn, Turn, Turn

Words Book of Ecclesiastes   Adaptation & music Pete Seeger

4/4 Rhythm/Arpeggio

See Course Book No. 1 Page 25.

Verse 2

A time to build up, a time to break down
A time to dance, a time to mourn
A time to cast away stones, a time to gather stones together.

Verse 3

A time of love, a time of hate
A time of war, a time of peace
A time you may embrace, a time to refrain from embracing.

Verse 4

A time to gain, a time to lose
A time to rend, a time to sew
A time to love, a time to hate
A time of peace, I swear it's not too late.

Wild Mountain Thyme
Arranged Russ Shipton

4/4 Rhythm/Arpeggio
See Course Book No. 1 Page 25.

Count: 1 & 2 & 3 & 4 &

Oh the sum-mer time is com-ing, _ and the trees are sweet-ly bloom-ing, _ and the

wild moun-tain thyme ___ grows a-round the bloom-ing hea-ther. _ Will you

CHORUS

go, lass-ie go? And we'll all go to-ge-ther, _ to pluck wild moun-tain

thyme _ all a-round the bloom-ing hea-ther. _ Will you go, lass-ie go?

Verse 2

I will build my love a tower near yon pure crystal fountain
And on it I will pile all the flowers of the mountain.

Verse 3

If my true love she were gone, I would surely find another
Where wild mountain thyme grows around the blooming heather.

The Sound Of Silence   Paul Simon

4/4 Rhythm/Arpeggio
See Course Book No. 1 Page 26.

Hel-lo dark-ness, my old friend, I've come to talk with you a - gain, be-cause a vis-ion soft-ly creep - ing, left its seeds while I was sleep - ing, and the vis - ion ___ that was plant-ed in my brain, still re - mains, with - in the sound of si - lence. ___

Verse 2

In restless dreams I walked alone
Narrow streets of cobblestone
'Neath the halo of a street lamp
I turned my collar to the cold and damp
When my eyes were stabbed by the flash of a neon light
That split the night and touched the sound of silence.

Verse 3

And in the naked light I saw
Ten thousand people maybe more
People talking without speaking
People hearing without listening
People writing songs that voices never share
And no one dare disturb the sound of silence.

Verse 4

'Fools,' said I, 'You do not know
Silence like a cancer grows
Hear my words that I might teach you
Take my arms that I might reach you.'
But my words like silent raindrops fell
And echoed in the wells of silence.

Verse 5

And the people bowed and prayed
To the neon god they made
And the sign flashed out its warning
In the words that it was forming
And the sign said 'The words of the prophets
Are written on the subway walls and tenement halls'
And whispered in the sounds of silence.

12

A Little Peace (Ein Bisschen Frieden)

Original German words
Bernd Meinunger
English words Paul Greedus
Music Ralph Siegel

4/4 Rhythm/Arpeggio

See Course Book No. 1 Page 28.

Verse 2

But then as I'm falling weighed down by the load
I picture a light at the end of the road
And closing my eyes I can see through the dark
The dream that is in my heart.

Chorus

A little loving, a little giving
To build a dream for the world we live in
A little patience and understanding
For our tomorrow, a little peace.

A little sunshine, a sea of gladness
To wash away all the tears of sadness
A little hoping, a little praying
For our tomorrow, a little peace;

Verse 3

I feel I'm a leaf in the November snow
I fell to the ground, there was no-one below
So now I am helpless alone with my song
Just wishing the storm was gone.

Lovesick Blues

Irving Mills & Clifford Friend

4/4 Rhythm/Strumming/Swing

See Course Book No. 2 Page 3.

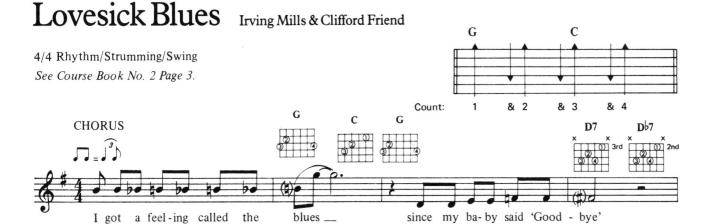

13

14

Careless Love   Arranged Russ Shipton

4/4 Rhythm/Strumming/Swing

See Course Book No. 2 Page 6.

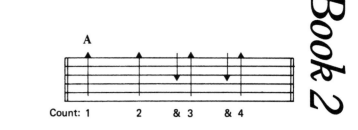

Count: 1   2   & 3   & 4

CHORUS (& VERSE)

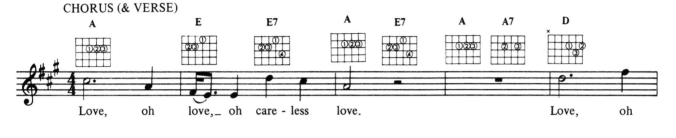

Love,   oh   love,_ oh care - less   love.   Love,   oh

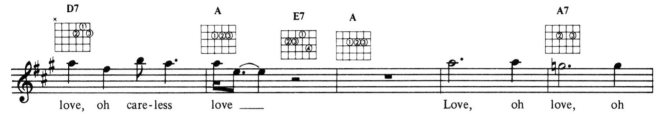

love, oh care-less   love _____   Love,   oh love,   oh

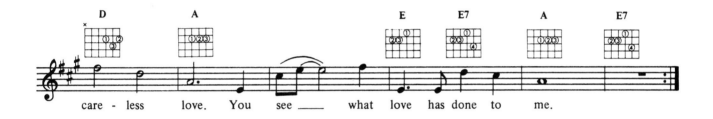

care - less   love. You   see _____ what   love   has done   to   me.

Verse 1 (melody as chorus)

What, oh what will mama say?
What, oh what will mama say?
What, oh what will mama say?
When she knows I've gone astray.

Verse 2

I love my mama and papa too
I love my mama and papa too
I love my mama and papa too
I'd leave them both to go with you.

Verse 3

Now you made me weep and you made me moan
You made me weep and you made me moan
You made me weep and you made me moan
Made me lose my happy home.

Verse 4

If I had listened to what she said
If I had heard what mama said
If I had heard what mama said
I'd still be home and in my bed.

Annie's Song   John Denver

3/4 Rhythm/Bass-strum
See Course Book No. 2 Page 9.

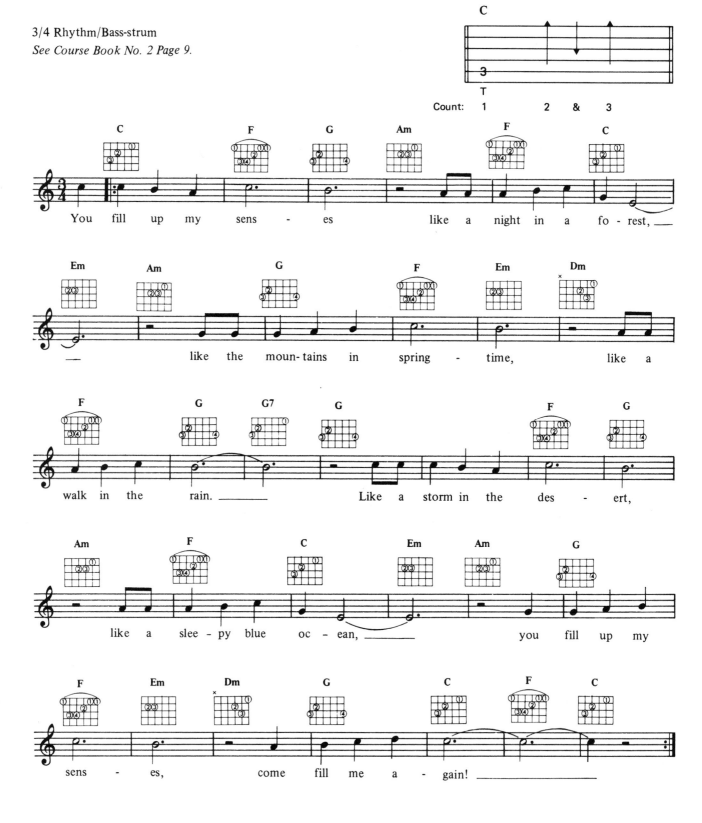

Count: 1   2 & 3

You fill up my sens - es like a night in a fo - rest, ___

___ like the moun- tains in spring - time, like a

walk in the rain. ___ Like a storm in the des - ert,

like a slee - py blue oc - ean, ___ you fill up my

sens - es, come fill me a - gain! ___

Verse 2

Come let me love you, let me give my life to you
Let me drown in your laughter, let me die in your arms
Let me lay down beside you, let me always be with you
Come let me love you, come love me again.

Ruby Don't Take Your Love To Town
Mel Tillis

Cut Time (4/4 with extra stress on 1st & 3rd beats)/Bass-strum
See Course Book No. 2 Page 10.

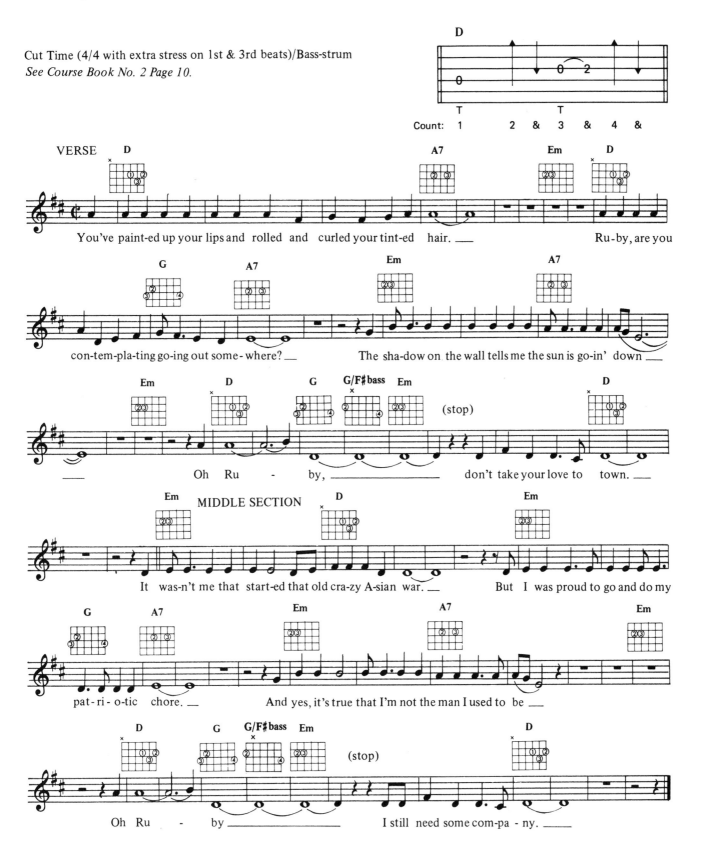

Verse 2

It's hard to love a man whose legs are bent and paralysed
And the wants and the needs of a woman your age
Ruby I realise
But it won't be long I've heard them say
Until I'm not around
Oh Ruby, don't take your love to town.

Verse 3

She's leavin' now 'cause I heard the slammin' of the door
The way I know I've heard it slam
One hundred times before
And if I could move I'd get my gun
And put her in the ground
Oh Ruby, for God's sake turn around!

The Mountains Of Mourne Arranged Russ Shipton

Book 2

6/8 Rhythm (roughly equivalent to two bars of 3/8)/
Arpeggio
See Course Book No. 2 Page 15.

Oh Ma-ry this Lon-don's a won-der-ful sight, with the peo-ple here work-ing by day and by night. They don't sow po-ta-toes nor bar-ley nor wheat, but there's gangs of them dig-gin' for gold in the street. At least when I asked them, that's what I was told, So I just took a hand at this dig-gin' for gold. But for all that I found there, I might as well be where the mount-ains of Mourne sweep down to the sea.

Verse 2

I believe that when writing a wish you expressed
As to how the fine ladies of London were dressed
Well if you believe me, when asked to a ball
They don't wear a top to their dresses at all
Oh I've seen them myself and you could not in truth
Say if they were bound for a ball or a bath
Don't be starting them fashions, now Mary McCree
Where the mountains of Mourne sweep down to the sea.

Verse 3

I've seen England's King from the top of a bus
I never knew him though he means to know us
And though by the Saxon we once were oppressed
Still I cheered, God forgive me, I cheered with the rest
And now that he's visited Erin's green shore
We'll be much better friends than we've been heretofore
When we've got all we want, we're as quiet as can be
Where the mountains of Mourne sweep down to the sea.

Verse 4

You remember young Peter O'Loughlin of course
Well now he is here at the head of the Force
I met him today, I was crossing the strand
And he stopped the whole street with one wave of his hand
And there we stood talking of days that are gone
While the whole population of London looked on
But for all his great powers, he's wishful, like me
To be back where the dark Mourne sweeps down to the sea.

Verse 5

There's beautiful girls here, oh never you mind
With beautiful shapes nature never designed
And lovely complexions, all roses and cream
But O'Loughlin remarked with regard to the same
That if at those roses you venture to sip
The colours might all come away on your lip
So I'll wait for the wild rose that's waiting for me
Where the mountains of Mourne sweep down to the sea.

18

The Trees They Do Grow High

Arranged Russ Shipton

4/4 Rhythm/Arpeggio
See Course Book No. 2 Page 18.

The trees they grow high, and the leaves they do grow green. Ma-ny is the
time my true ___ love I've seen. Ma-ny an hour I've
watched him all a - lone. He's young but he's dai-ly ___ grow-ing. ___

Verse 2

Father, dear father, you've done me great wrong
You've married me to a boy who's much too young
I am twice twelve and he is but fourteen
He's young but he's daily growing.

Verse 3

Daughter, dear daughter, I've done you no wrong
I have married you to a great Lord's son
He'll make a Lord for you to wait upon
He's young but he's daily growing.

Verse 4

Father, dear father, if you see fit
We'll send him to college for one year yet
I'll tie blue ribbons all around his head
To let the maidens know that he's married.

Verse 5

One day I was looking o'er my father's castle wall
I spied all the boys a-playin' with the ball
My own true love was the flower of them all
He's young but he's daily growing.

Verse 6

At the age of fourteen he was a married man
At the age of fifteen the father of a son
At the age of sixteen his grave it was green
And death had put an end to his growing.

I Can't Help But Wonder (Where I'm Bound)

Tom Paxton

Cut Time Rhythm (4/4 with extra stress on 1st & 3rd beats)/Alternating Thumb
See Course Book No. 2 Page 22.

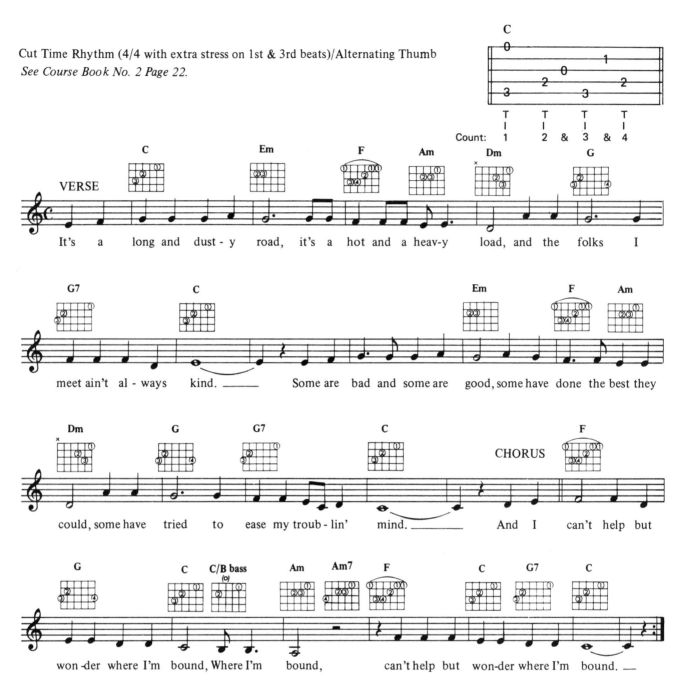

Verse 2

I have wandered through this land
Just a-doin' the best I can
Tryin' to find what I was meant to do
And the people that I see
Look as worried as can be
And it looks like they are a-wonderin' too.

Verse 3

I had a little girl one time
She had lips like cherry wine
And she loved me till my head went plumb insane
But I was too blind to see
She was driftin' away from me
And my good gal went off on the mornin' train.

Verse 4

And I had a buddy back home
But he started out to roam
And I hear he's out by 'Frisco Bay
And sometimes when I've had a few
His old voice comes singin' through
And I'm goin' out to see him some old day.

Verse 5

If you see me passin' by
And you stop and you wonder why
And you wish that you were a rambler too
Nail your shoes to the kitchen floor
Lace 'em up and bar the door
Thank your stars for the roof that's over you.

My Ramblin' Boy
Tom Paxton

Cut Time (4/4 with extra stress on 1st & 3rd beats)/
Alternating thumb

See Course Book No. 2 Page 22.

VERSE

He was a man   and a friend al - ways.   He stuck with me   in the hard old   days.

He nev-er cared   if I had no dough.   We ram-bled round   in the rain and snow

CHORUS

And here's to   you,   my ramb-lin' boy.   May all your   ramb - lin' bring you joy.

And here's to you,   my ramb-lin' boy.   May all your   ramb - lin' bring you joy.

Verse 2

In Tulsa town we chanced to stray
We thought we'd try to work one day
The boss said he had room for one
Says my old pal 'We'd rather bum'.

Verse 3

Late one night in a jungle camp
The weather it was cold and damp
He got the chills and he got 'em bad
They took the only friend I had.

Verse 4

He left me here to ramble on
My ramblin' pal is dead and gone
If when we die we go somewhere
I'll bet you a dollar he's ramblin' there.

Everybody's Talkin' Fred Neil

4/4 Rhythm/Alternating thumb
See Course Book No. 2 Page 26.

Ev-'ry-bod-y's talk-in' at me, I don't hear a word they're say-in', on-ly the

ech-oes of my mind. Peo-ple stop-pin', star-in', I can't

see their fac-es, on-ly the sha-dows of their eyes. I'm go-in' where the

sun keeps shin-in' through the pour-in' rain, go-in' where the wea-ther suits my

clothes, _____ bank-ing off of the North East wind,— sail-in' on sum-mer

breeze, and skip-pin' ov-er the oc-ean __ like a stone.

ENDING

And I won't let you leave my love be-hind. _____ No

Midnight Special Arranged Russ Shipton

4/4 Rhythm/Strumming
See Course Book No. 3 Page 4.

Count: 1   2 & 3 & 4 &

Well you wake up in the morn-ing, __ hear the ding dong ring, __ and you go march-in' to the

ta - ble,   see the same damn thing, knife and fork up-on the ta - ble __ but there's no-thin' in the

pan, __   and if you say some-thin' a-bout it: you're in trou-ble with the man! Let the mid-night

CHORUS

(stop)

spe-cial shine her light on me.   Let the mid-night spe-cial __ shine her ev-er lov-in' light on me!

Verse 2

Yonder comes Miss Rosie, how in the world do you know?
I can tell her by her apron and the dress she wore
Umbrella on her shoulder, piece of paper in her hand
She goes marching to the captain, says 'I want my man!'

Verse 3

Yonder comes Doctor Melton, how in the world do you know?
Well he gave me a tablet just the day before
Now there never was a doctor anywhere in this land
That could ever cure the fever of a convict man!

Verse 4

Well if you ever go to Houston, you better walk right
You better not stagger, and you better not fight
Sheriff Benson will arrest you, yeah he'll send you down
The jury finds you guilty, you'll be sugarland bound!

Yesterday   John Lennon & Paul McCartney

4/4 Rhythm/Strumming/Double time

See Course Book No. 3 Page 4.

Count: 1   2 & 3 & 4 &

VERSE

Yes-ter-day,   all my trou-bles seemed so far a-way,   now it looks as tho' they're

here to stay,   oh I be-lieve in yes-ter-day.

MIDDLE SECTION

Why she had to go I don't know, she would-n't say.

I said some-thing wrong, now I long for yes-ter-day._____

Verse 2

Suddenly, I'm not half the man I used to be
There's a shadow hanging over me
Oh yesterday came suddenly

Verse 3

Yesterday, love was such an easy game to play
Now I need a place to hide away
Oh I believe in yesterday.

Bridge Over Troubled Water
Paul Simon

4/4 Rhythm/Strumming/Double time
See Course Book No. 3 Page 5.

When you're wea - ry, feel - in' small, when tears are in your eyes I'll dry them all. _____ I'm on your side. Oh, when times get rough, and friends just can't be found, like a bridge ov - er trou-bled wat - er, I will lay me down, like a bridge ov - er trou - bled wat - er, I will lay me down.

Verse 2

When you're down and out
When you're on the street
When evening falls so hard
I will comfort you
I'll take your part
Oh when darkness comes
And pain is all around
Like a bridge over troubled water
I will lay me down
Like a bridge over troubled water
I will lay me down.

Verse 3

Sail on silver girl, sail on by
Your time has come to shine
All your dreams are on their way
See how they shine
Oh if you need a friend
I'm sailing right behind
Like a bridge over troubled water
I will ease your mind
Like a bridge over troubled water
I will ease your mind.

25

Daniel
Elton John & Bernie Taupin

4/4 Rhythm/Strumming
See Course Book No. 3 Page 6.

Verse 2

They say Spain is pretty though I've never been
Well Daniel says it's the best place he's ever seen
Oh and he should know, he's been there enough
Lord I miss Daniel, oh I miss him so much.

Killing Me Softly With His Song

Words Norman Gimble
Music Charles Fox

4/4 Rhythm/Strumming
See Course Book No. 3 Page 6.

Verse 1 lyrics (under music):
I heard he sang a good song; I heard he had a style. And so I came to see him to lis-ten for a while. And there he was this young boy, a stran-ger to my eyes. strum-ming my pain with his fin-gers, sing-ing my life with his words. Kill-ing me soft-ly with his song, kill-ing me soft-ly, with his song, tell-ing my whole life with his words, kill-ing me soft-ly, with his song.

Verse 2

I felt all flushed with fever, embarrassed by the crowd
I felt he'd found my letters and read each one out loud
I prayed that he would finish but he just kept right on
Strumming my pain with his fingers
Singing my life with his words
Killing me softly with his song
Killing me softly with his song
Telling my whole life with his words
Killing me softly with his song.

Verse 3

He sang as if he knew me, in all my dark despair
And then he looked right through me as if I wasn't there
But he was there this stranger, singing clear and strong
Strumming my pain with his fingers
Singing my life with his words
Killing me softly with his song
Killing me softly with his song
Telling my whole life with his words
Killing me softly with his song.

Year Of The Cat
Al Stewart & Peter Wood

Book 3

4/4 Rhythm/Strumming
See Course Book No. 3 Page 6.

VERSE

On a morn-ing from a Bo-gart mov-ie, in a count-ry where they turn back time, you go

strol-lin' through the crowd like Pe-ter Lor-re con-tem-pla-ting a crime. She comes out of the sun in a

silk dress, run-nin' like a wa-ter-col-our in the rain. Don't bo-ther ask-ing for

ex-pla-na-tions, she'll just tell you that she came in the year of the cat. (2. She)

MIDDLE SECTION

Well she looks at you so cool-ly, and her eyes shine like the moon and the sea. She comes in

in-cense and patch-ou-li, so you take her to find what's wait-ing in-

side. The year of the cat. (3. Well)

Verse 2

She doesn't give you time for questions
As she locks up your arm in hers
And you follow till your sense of direction completely disappears
By the blue-tiled walls near the market stalls
There's a hidden door she leads you to
These days she says, I feel my life just like a river
Running through the year of the cat.

Verse 3

Well morning comes and you're still with her
And the bus and the tourists are gone
And you've thrown away your choice
And lost your ticket so you have to stay on
But the drum beat strains of the night remain
In the rhythm of the new-born day
You know sometime you're bound to leave her
But for now you're gonna stay in the year of the cat.

28

Nine Pound Hammer Arranged Russ Shipton

Cut Time (4/4 with extra stress on 1st & 3rd)/
Alternating thumb/Swing
See Course Book No. 3 Page 20.

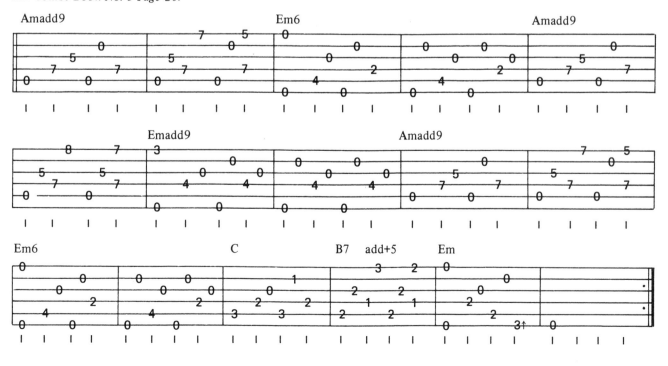

This nine pound ham-mer, is a lit-tle too hea-vy, for my size, yes for my size.

Verse 2

So I'm goin' to the mountain to see my baby
And I ain't comin' back, no I ain't comin' back.

Verse 3

Won't you roll on buddy, don't you roll so slow
Tell me how can I roll, roll, roll, when the wheels won't go?

Verse 4

Won't you roll on buddy, you who're rollin' coal
How can I roll, roll, roll, when the wheels won't go?

Verse 5

When I die, you can make my tombstone
Out of number nine coal, out of number nine coal.

Road To Nowhere Russ Shipton

4/4 Rhythm/Alternating thumb
See Course Book No. 3 Page 20.

Kansas City

Jerry Lieber and Mike Stoller

4/4 Rhythm/Strumming/Swing
See Course Book No. 4 Page 9.

Verse 2

Now I'll be standin' on the corner, twelfth street and Vine
Yeah I'll be standin' on the corner, twelfth street and Vine
With my Kansas City baby and my bottle of cherry wine.

Verse 3

Well I may take a train, might take a plane
If I have to walk I'm gonna get there just the same
I'm goin' to Kansas City, Kansas City here I come
They got some crazy little women there
And I'm gonna have me some!

30

That'll Be The Day

Norman Petty, Buddy Holly & Jerry Allison

4/4 Rhythm/Strumming/Swing/Damping

See Course Book No. 4 Page 9.

VERSE

Well you give me all your lov-in' and your tur-tle dov-in', all your hugs and kiss-es and your mon-ey too, well, you know you love me ba-by, un-til you tell me, may-be, that some day, well I'll be through. Well __

CHORUS

that-'ll be the day, when you say good-bye, yes __ that-'ll be the day, when you make me cry. Oh you say you're gon-na leave, you know it's a lie 'cause that-'ll be the day _____ when I die!

Verse 2

When Cupid shot his dart he shot it at your heart
So if we ever part and I leave you
You say you told me and you told me boldly
That someday well I'll be through.

The Fifty-Ninth Street Bridge Song
(Feelin' Groovy) Paul Simon

4/4 Rhythm/Alternating thumb/Swing
See Course Book No. 4 Page 11.

VERSES 1 & 2

Slow down,_you move too fast. ___ You got to make the morn-ing last, just kick-in' down _ the

cobb-le - stones,_ look-in' for fun and feel-in' groo - vy. _____

LAST VERSE

Got no deeds to do, no prom-i-ses to keep; I'm dapp-led and drow-sy and

read - y to sleep; let the morn-ing time drop all its pet-als on me.

Life, I love you, all is groo - vy!

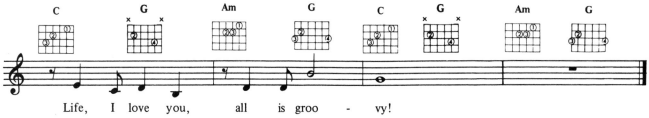

Verse 2

Hello lamppost, watcha knowing?
I've come to watch your flowers growing
Ain't cha got no rhymes for me?
Doot-in doo-doo, feelin' groovy.

Not Fade Away
Charles Hardin & Norman Petty

Book 4

4/4 Rhythm/Strumming/Damping
See Course Book No. 4 Page 9

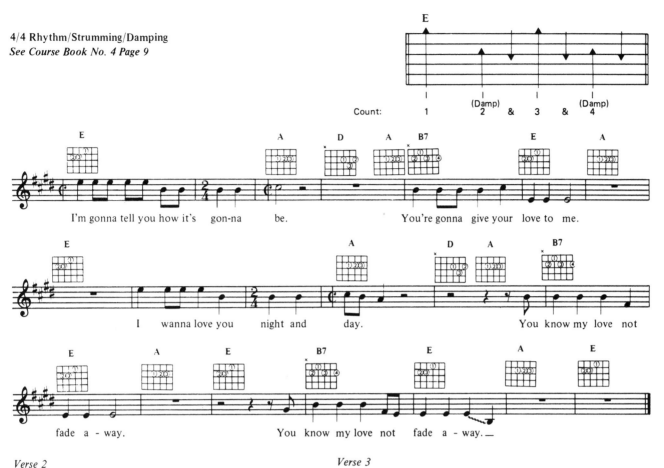

I'm gonna tell you how it's gon-na be. You're gonna give your love to me.

I wanna love you night and day. You know my love not

fade a-way. You know my love not fade a-way.

Verse 2

My love is bigger than a Cadillac
I try to show it and you drive me back
Your love for me has got to be real
For you to know just how I feel
A love for real not fade away.

Verse 3

I'm gonna tell you how it's gonna be
You're gonna give-a your love to me
A love to last more than one day
A love that's love not fade away
A love that's love not fade away.

© 1957 MPL COMMUNICATIONS, INC. and WREN MUSIC CO.
International Copyright Secured.   All Rights Reserved.

Marco
Russ Shipton

4/4 Rhythm/Alternating Thumb/Pull-offs
See Course Book No. 4 Page 12.

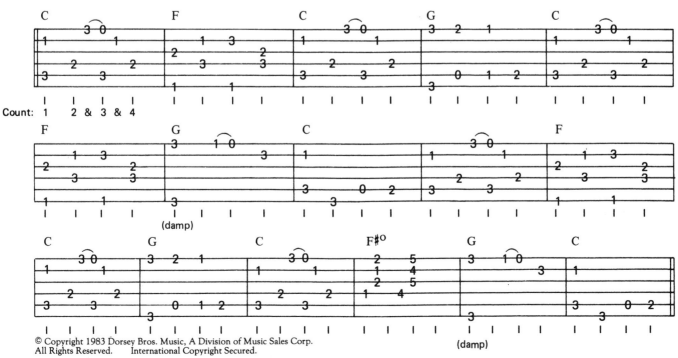

© Copyright 1983 Dorsey Bros. Music, A Division of Music Sales Corp.
All Rights Reserved.   International Copyright Secured.

33

Gone Fishing Russ Shipton

4/4 Rhythm/Monotonic Bass and Alternating Thumb/
Hammer-ons, Pull-offs, Slides and Harmonics (12˙ = harmonic at 12th fret)
See Course Book No. 4 Page 15.

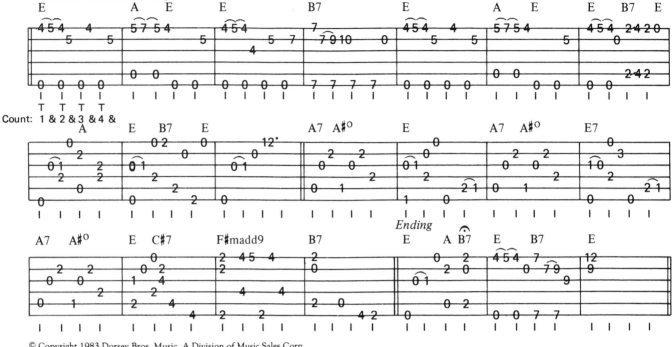

Night Breeze Russ Shipton

4/4 Rhythm/Monotonic Bass and Alternating Thumb mixed/
Slides, Hammer-ons, Pull offs, Bends and Harmonics/Swing (12˙ = harmonic at 12th fret)
See Course Book No. 4 Page 15.

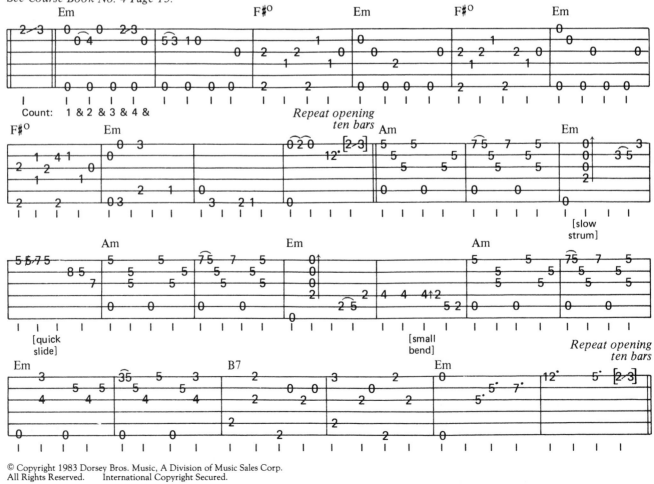

34

Out Near Alice Russ Shipton

4/4 Rhythm/Monotonic Bass and Strumming styles/
Harmonics (12˙ = harmonic at 12th fret)
See Course Book No. 4 Page 15.

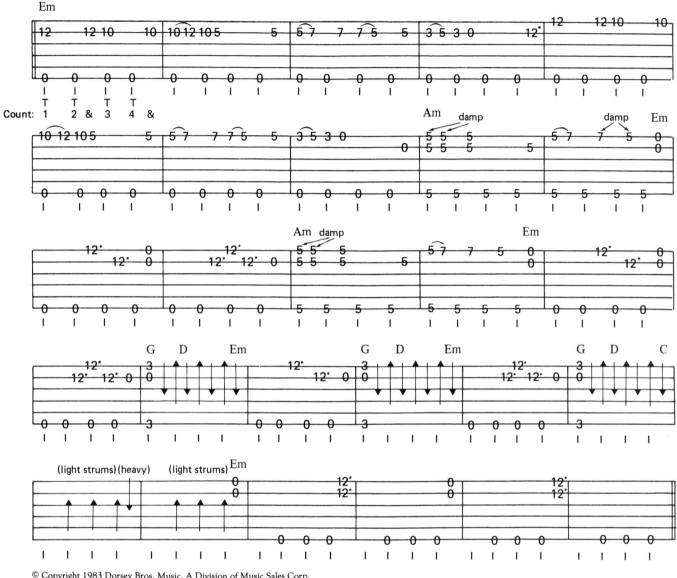

© Copyright 1983 Dorsey Bros. Music, A Division of Music Sales Corp.
All Rights Reserved.   International Copyright Secured.

Skimatics Russ Shipton

Cut Time (4/4 with extra stress on 1st and 3rd beats)/Monotonic Bass and Runs/
Hammer-ons and Slides/Swing (3 notes in one beat should be played as a triplet)
See Course Book No. 4 Page 18.

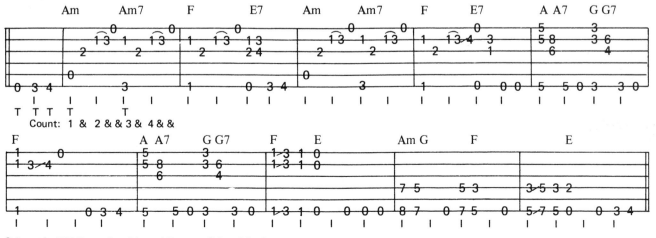

© Copyright 1983 Dorsey Bros. Music, A Division of Music Sales Corp.
All Rights Reserved.   International Copyright Secured.

M.T.A.   Russ Shipton

3/8 Rhythm/Arpeggio with changing Bass
See Course Book No. 4 Page 18.

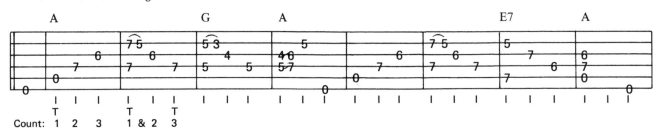

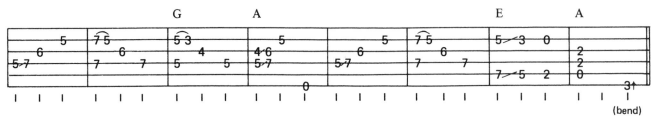

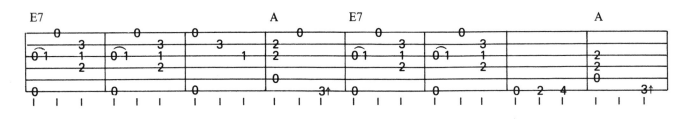

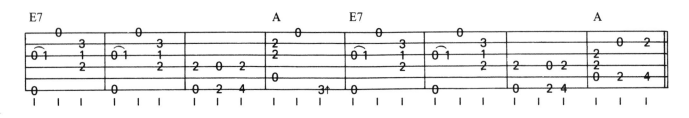

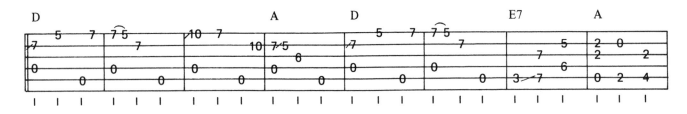

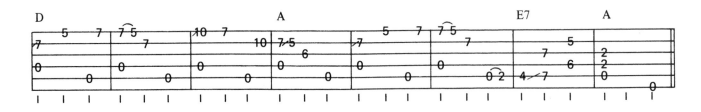

Ending

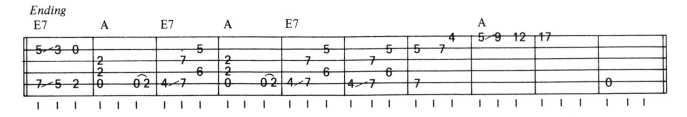

36

D'Arcy Farrow   Arranged Russ Shipton

4/4 Rhythm/Alternating thumb
(6th string tuned down one tone to D)
See Course Book No. 4 Page 20.

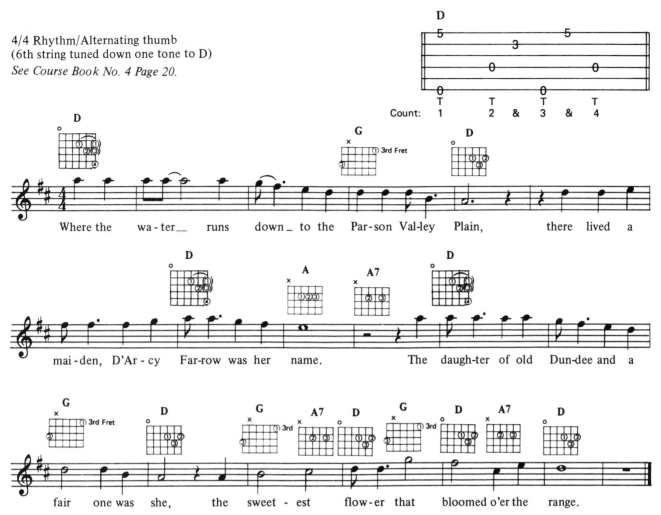

Where the wa-ter__ runs down__ to the Par-son Val-ley Plain, there lived a mai-den, D'Ar-cy Far-row was her name. The daugh-ter of old Dun-dee and a fair one was she, the sweet-est flow-er that bloomed o'er the range.

Verse 2

Her voice was as sweet as sugar candy
Her touch was as soft as a bed of goose down
Her eyes shone bright like the pretty lights
That shine in the night out of Yellington town.

Verse 3

She was courted by a young man, Dandy Hare
A fine lad was he, as I am to hear
He gave her silver rings and lacy things
And he promised to wed before the snows came that year.

Verse 4

Her pony it stumbled and she did fall
Her dying touched the hearts of us one and all
Young Dandy in his pain put a bullet through his brain
We buried them together as the snow began to fall.

Verse 5

They sang of D'Arcy Farrow where the Truckee runs through
They sing of her beauty in Virginia City too
At dusky sundown to her name they drink a round
And to young Dandy whose love was true.

Madeleine Russ Shipton

3/4 Rhythm/Syncopated Arpeggio (stress notes
with asterisk above to bring out melody properly)
See Course Book No. 4 Page 21.

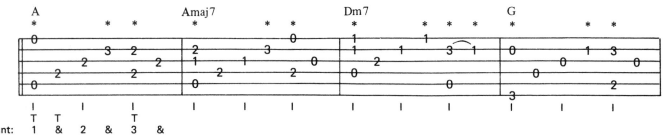

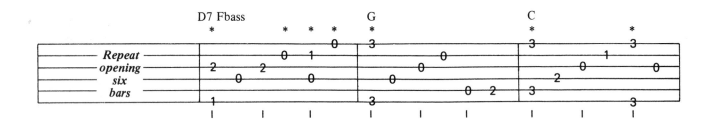

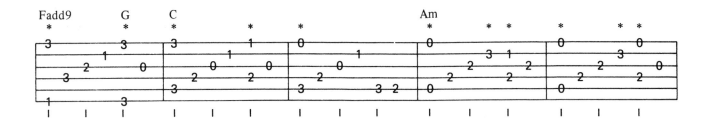

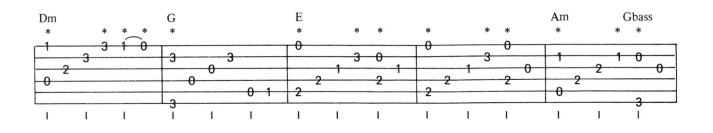

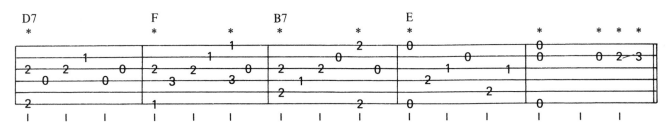

38

Blackbird John Lennon & Paul McCartney

Cut Time (4/4 with extra stress on 1st and 3rd beats)/Alternating Thumb and pinch-pluck mixed

See Course Book No. 4 Page 21.

MIDDLE SECTION

Verse 2

Blackbird singing in the dead of night
Take these sunken eyes and learn to see
All your life
You were only waiting for this moment to be free.

Royal Dance · Russ Shipton

3/4 Rhythm/Moving Bass line (the bass is the melody and should be emphasised)
See Course Book No. 4 Page 26.

40

The Complete Guitar Player Songbook No. 4

by Russ Shipton

Amsco Publications
New York/London/Sydney

Amsco Publications
New York/London/Sydney

Music Sales Corporation
225 Park Avenue South, New York, NY 10003 USA

Music Sales Limited
8/9 Frith Street, London W1V 5TZ England

Music Sales Pty. Limited
120 Rothschild Street, Rosebery, Sydney, NSW 2018, Australia

International Standard Book Number: 0.8256.2342.1

Printed in the United States of America by
Vicks Lithograph and Printing Corporation

You've Got To Hide Your Love Away

John Lennon & Paul McCartney

12/8 Rhythm/Strumming
See Course Book No. 1 Page 6

VERSE

Here I stand, with head in hand, ___ turn my face to the wall.

If she's gone, I can't go on, ___ feel-ing two feet small. _____

Ev'-ry-where, peo-ple stare, — each and — ev'-ry day. I can see them laugh at me, —

and I hear them say: _____

CHORUS

Hey, you've got to hide your love a -

way! _____ Hey, you've got to hide your love a - way! _____

Verse 2

How can I even try, I can never win
Hearing them, seeing them, in the state I'm in
How could she say to me, love will find a way
Gather round all you clowns, let me hear you say:

Let It Be John Lennon & Paul McCartney

Cut time/Strumming
See Course Book No. 1 Page 12

Middle Chorus (2nd line)
There will be an answer, let it be.

Verse 2

And when the broken-hearted people
Living in the world agree
There will be an answer, let it be
For though they may be parted
There is still a chance that they will see
There will be an answer, let it be.

Verse 3

And when the night is cloudy
There is still a light that shines on me
Shine until tomorrow, let it be
I wake up to the sound of music
Mother Mary comes to me
Speaking words of wisdom, let it be.

The Night They Drove Old Dixie Down   J. Robbie Robertson

4/4 Rhythm/Strumming
See Course Book No. 1 Page 12

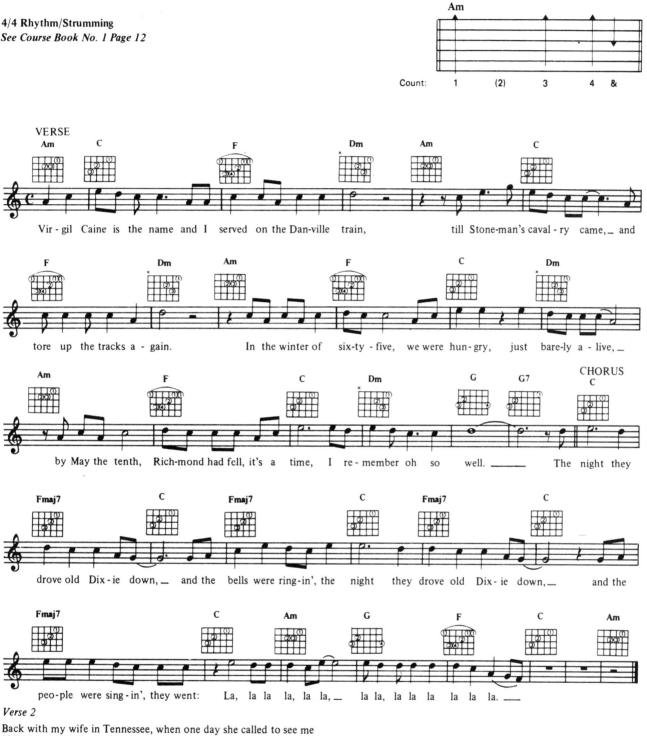

Count: 1   (2)   3   4   &

VERSE

Vir - gil Caine is the name and I served on the Dan-ville train, till Stone-man's caval - ry came,_ and

tore up the tracks a - gain. In the winter of six-ty - five, we were hun-gry, just bare-ly a - live,_

by May the tenth, Rich-mond had fell, it's a time, I re-member oh so well. _____ The night they

drove old Dix - ie down,_ and the bells were ring-in', the night they drove old Dix - ie down,_ and the

peo-ple were sing-in', they went: La, la la la, la la,_ la la, la la la la la la la.___

Verse 2

Back with my wife in Tennessee, when one day she called to see me
"Virgil quick come see, there goes Robert E. Lee!"
Now I don't mind choppin' wood, and I don't care if the money's no good
Just take what you need and leave the rest
But they should never have taken the very best.

Verse 3

Like my father before me I will work the land
And like my brother above me who took a rebel stand
He was just eighteen, proud and brave, but a yankee laid him in his grave
I swear by the mud below my feet
You can't raise a Caine back up when he's in defeat.

Little Boxes   Malvina Reynolds

3/4 Rhythm/Bass-pluck/Swing
See Course Book No. 1 Page 20

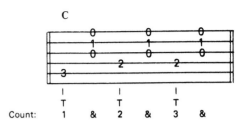

Count: 1   &   2   &   3   &

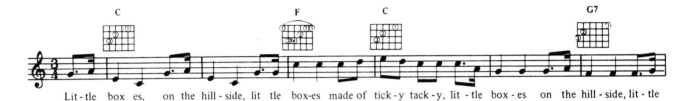

Lit - tle box es,   on the hill - side, lit tle box-es made of tick-y tack-y, lit - tle box - es   on the hill - side, lit - tle

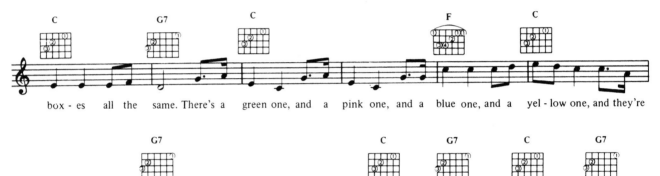

box - es   all the   same. There's a   green one, and a   pink one, and a   blue one, and a   yel - low one, and they're

all made out of tick-y tack-y, and they all   look just the   same.

Verse 2

And the people in the houses
All went to the University
Where they were put in boxes
And they came out all the same
And there's doctors and there's lawyers
And business executives
And they're all made out of ticky tacky
And they all look just the same.

Verse 3

And they all play on the golf course
And drink their martinis dry
And they all have pretty children
And the children go to school
And the children go to summer camp
And then to the university
Where they are put in boxes
And they come out all the same.

Verse 4

And the boys go into business
And marry and raise a family
And they all get put in boxes
Little boxes all the same
There's a green one and a pink one
And a blue one and a yellow one
And they're all made out of ticky tacky
And they all look just the same.

Mrs McGrath   Arranged Russ Shipton

Cut time/Bass-strum
See Course Book No. 1 Page 20

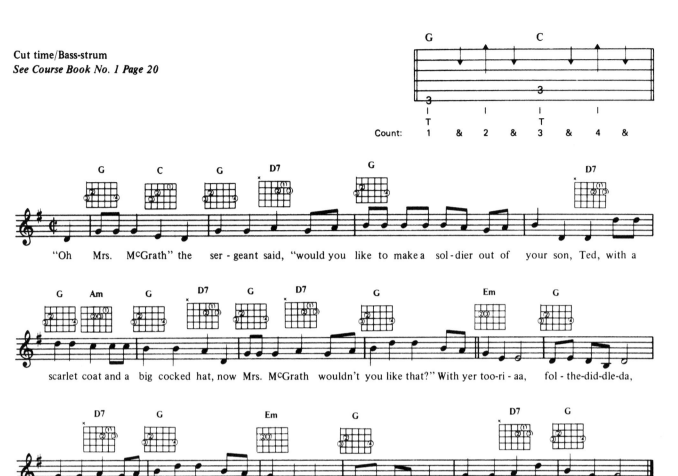

Count: 1 & 2 & 3 & 4 &

"Oh   Mrs. McGrath" the   ser - geant said, "would you like to make a sol - dier out of   your son, Ted, with a

scarlet coat and a big cocked hat, now Mrs. McGrath wouldn't you like that?" With yer too-ri - aa,   fol - the-did-dle-da,

too-ri - oo - ri ___ oo- ri - aa, with yer too- ri - aa,   fol - the-did-dle - da,   too - ri - oo - ri   oo - ri - aa.

Verse 2

Well Mrs McGrath lived on the seashore
For the space of seven long years or more
Till she saw a big ship sailing into the bay
"Here's my son Ted, will ya clear the way?".

Verse 3

"Oh Captain, dear, where have you been?"
"Have you been sailing on the mediterreen?"
"And have you any tidings of my son, Ted?"
"Is the poor boy living, or is he dead?".

Verse 4

Then up comes Ted without any legs
And in their place he has two wooden pegs
She kissed him a dozen times or two
Saying "Holy Moses, sure it can't be you!"

Verse 5

"Oh then were you drunk or were you blind"
"That you left your two fine legs behind?"
"Or was it waliking upon the sea"
"Wore your two fine legs from the knees away?"

Verse 6

"Well I wasn't drunk and I wasn't blind"
"When I left my two fine legs behind"
"For a cannon ball on the fifth of May"
"Took my two fine legs from the knees away!"

Verse 7

"Oh then Teddy me boy," the widow cried
"Yer two fine legs were yer mammy's pride
Them stumps of a tree wouldn't do at all
Why didn't yer run from the big cannon ball?"

Verse 8

"Well all foreign wars I do proclaim
Between Don John and the King of Spain
And by herrins I'll make them rue the time
That they swept the legs from a child of mine!"

Verse 9

"Oh then if I had you back again
I'd never let you go to fight the King of Spain
For I'd rather have my Ted as he used to be
Than the King of France and his whole Navy!"

Quare Bungle Rye   Arranged Russ Shipton

3/4 Rhythm/Bass-strum
See Course Book No. 1 Page 20

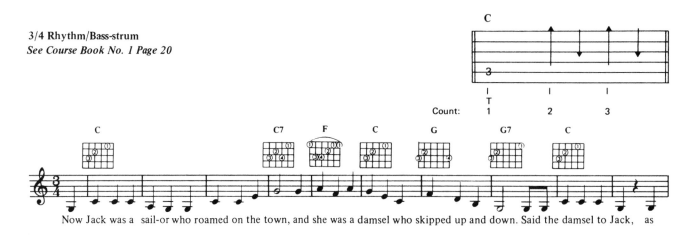

Count: 1   2   3

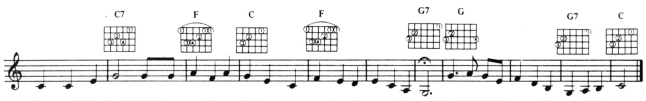

Now Jack was a sail-or who roamed on the town, and she was a damsel who skipped up and down. Said the damsel to Jack,   as

she passed him by: "Would you care for to purchase some quare bungle rye, raddy rye?" Fol the diddle rye raddy rye raddy rye.

Verse 2
Thought Jack to himself, now what can this be?
But the finest of whiskey from far Germany
Smuggled up in a basket and sold on the sly
And the name that it goes by is quare bungle rye, raddy rye
Fol the diddle rye raddy, rye raddy rye.

Verse 3
Jack gave her a pound and thought nothing strange
Said she hold the basket till I get your change
Jack looked in the basket and a baby did spy
Oh begorrah says Jack, this is quare bungle rye, raddy rye
Fol the diddle rye raddy, ryr raddy rye.

Verse 4
Now to get the child christened was Jack's first intent
And to get the child christened to the parson he went
Said the parson to Jack, what will he go by?
Bedad now says Jack, this is quare bungle rye, raddy rye
Fol the diddle rye raddy, rye raddy rye.

Verse 5
Says the parson to Jack, now that's a queer name
Says Jack to the parson, t'was a queer way he came
Smuggled up in a basket and sold on the sly
And the name that he went by was quare bungle rye, raddy rye
Fol the diddle rye raddy, rye raddy rye.

Verse 6   Now all you young sailors who roam on the town
Beware of the damsel who skips up and down
Take a look in the basket as she passes you by
Or else they may pawn on you quare bungle rye, raddy rye
Fol the diddle rye raddy, rye raddy rye.

Six Nights Drunk   Arranged Russ Shipton

2/4 Rhythm/Bass-pluck/Swing
See Course Book No. 1 Page 20

VERSE

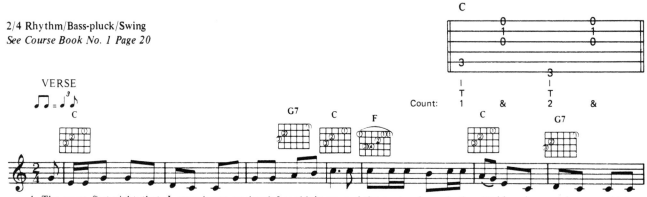

Count: 1   &   2   &

1. The ve-ry first night that I came home, so drunk I couldn't see, and there was a horse in the sta-ble, where my horse ought to

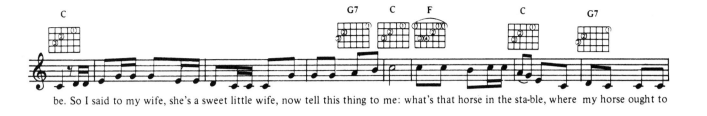

be. So I said to my wife, she's a sweet little wife, now tell this thing to me: what's that horse in the sta-ble, where my horse ought to

CHORUS

be? You're drunk you're drunk you silly old fool, so drunk you cannot see, it's nothing but a milking cow my mother sent to

me. Well it's many a day I've travelled — a hundred miles or more, but a sad-dle on a milk-ing cow I've never seen be-fore!

Verse 2

Now the very next night that I came home
So drunk I couldn't see
And there was a coat on the coatstand
Where my coat ought to be
So I said to my wife, she's a sweet little wife
Now tell this thing to me
What's that coat on the coatstand
Where my coat ought to be?

Chorus (3rd & 6th lines)

It's nothing but a blanket that my mother sent to me
But buttons on a blanket I have never seen before!

Verse 3

Now the very next night that I came home
So drunk I couldn't see
And there was a hat on the hat-rack
Where my hat ought to be
So I said to my wife, she's a sweet little wife
Now tell this thing to me
What's that hat on the hat-rack
Where my hat ought to be?

Chorus (3rd & 6th lines)

It's nothing but a chamber pot my mother sent to me
But a chamber pot size six and seven eights
I have never seen before!

Verse 4

Now the very next night that I came home
So drunk I couldn't see
And there were boots under the bed
Where my boots ought to be
So I said to my wife, she's a sweet little wife
Now tell this thing to me
What's these boots under the bed wh
Where my boots ought to be?

Chorus (3rd & 6th lines)

It's nothing but two marrows that my mother sent to me
But laces on a marrow I have never seen before!

Verse 5

Now the very next night that I came home
So drunk I couldn't see
And there were trousers on the bed
Where my trousers ought to be
So I said to my wife, she's a sweet little wife
Now tell this thing to me
What's these trousers on the bed
Where my trousers ought to be?

Chorus (3rd & 6th lines)

It's nothing but a little flag my mother sent to me
But flies upon a Union Jack I've never seen before!

Verse 6

Now the very next night that I came home
So drunk I couldn't see
And there was a head on the pillow
Where my head ought to be
So I said to my wife, she's a sweet little wife
Now tell this thing to me
What's that head there on the bed
Where my head ought to be?

Chorus (3rd & 6th lines)

It's nothing but a baby that my mother sent to me
But a moustache on a baby I have never seen before!

Rocky Mountain High

John Denver & Mike Taylor

4/4 Rhythm/Bass-strum
See Course Book No. 1 Page 20

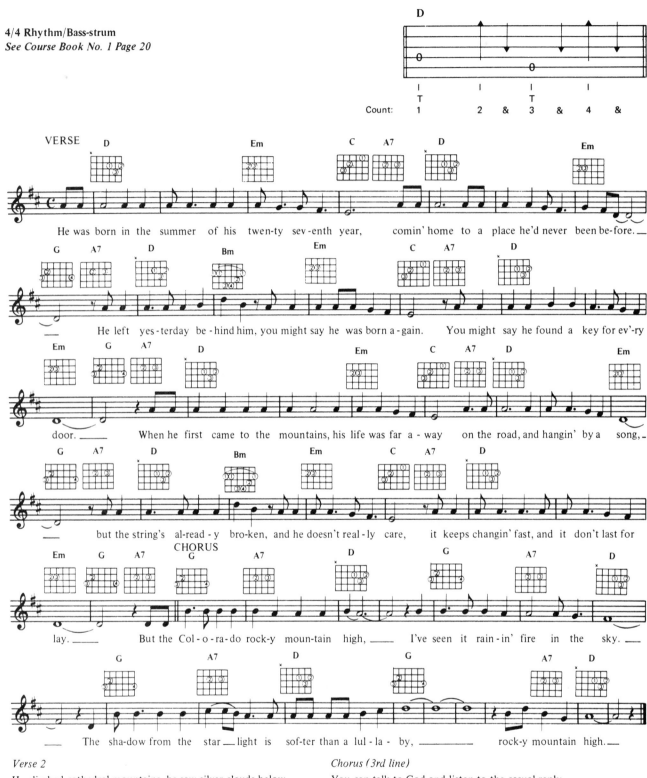

VERSE

He was born in the summer of his twen-ty sev-enth year, comin' home to a place he'd never been be-fore.

He left yes-terday be-hind him, you might say he was born a-gain. You might say he found a key for ev'-ry

door. When he first came to the mountains, his life was far a-way on the road, and hangin' by a song,

but the string's al-read-y bro-ken, and he doesn't real-ly care, it keeps changin' fast, and it don't last for

CHORUS

lay. But the Col-o-ra-do rock-y moun-tain high, I've seen it rain-in' fire in the sky.

The sha-dow from the star light is sof-ter than a lul-la-by, rock-y mountain high.

Verse 2

He climbed cathedral mountains, he saw silver clouds below
He saw everything as far as you can see
And they say that he got crazy once, and he tried to touch the sun
And he lost a friend but kept his memory
Now he walks in quiet solitude, the forests and the streams
Seeking grace in every step he takes
His sight has turned inside himself to try and understand
The serenity of a clear blue mountain lake.

Chorus (3rd line)

You can talk to God and listen to the casual reply

Verse 3

Now his life is full of wonder but his heart still knows some fear
Of a simple thing he cannot comprehend
Why they try to tear the mountains down to bring in a couple more
More people, more scars upon the land.

Chorus (3rd line)

I know he'd be a poorer man if he never saw an eagle fly

The Whistling Gypsy Rover

Arranged Russ Shipton

4/4 Rhythm/Arpeggio
See Course Book No. 1 Page 25

The gyp-sy rov-er came ov-er the hill, down through the val-ley so sha-dy. He whist-led and he sang till the green-woods rang, and he won the heart of a la-dy.

Verse 2

She left her father's castle gate
She left her own true lover
She left her servants and her estate
To follow the gypsy rover.

Verse 3

Her father saddled up his fastest steed
And roamed the valleys all over
He sought his daughter at great speed
And the whistling gypsy rover.

Verse 4

He came at last to a mansion fine
Down by the river Clady
And there was music and there was wine
For the gypsy and his lady.

Verse 5

He is no gypsy, father said she
But Lord of these lands all over
And I shall stay till my dying day
With my whistling gypsy rover.

Can't Help Falling In Love

George Weiss, Hugo Peretti & Luigi Creatore

4/4 Rhythm (12/8 feel)/Arpeggio
See Course Book No. 1 Page 28

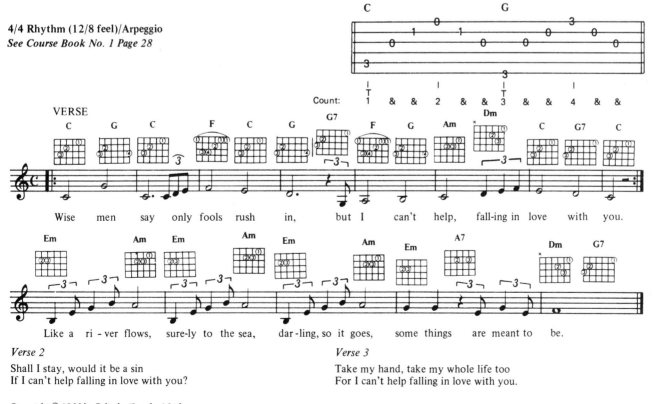

Wise men say only fools rush in, but I can't help, fall-ing in love with you.

Like a ri-ver flows, sure-ly to the sea, dar-ling, so it goes, some things are meant to be.

Verse 2

Shall I stay, would it be a sin
If I can't help falling in love with you?

Verse 3

Take my hand, take my whole life too
For I can't help falling in love with you.

Plaisir D'Amour   Arranged Russ Shipton

3/4 Rhythm/Arpeggio
See Course Book No. 1 Page 28

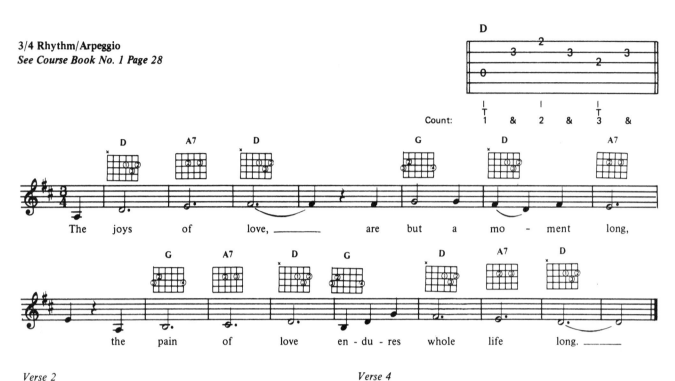

The joys of love, _____ are but a mo-ment long,

the pain of love en-du-res whole life long. _____

Verse 2

Your eyes kissed mine, I saw a love in them shine
You brought me heaven on earth when your eyes kissed mine.

Verse 3

My love loves me, and all the wonders I see
A rainbow shines in my window when my love loves me.

Verse 4

And now he's gone, like a dream that fades into dawn
But the world stays locked in my heartstrings, my love loves me.

Verse 5

Plaisir d'amour, ne dure qu'un moment
Chagrin d'amour dure toute la vie.

The Curragh Of Kildare   Arranged Russ Shipton

4/4 Rhythm/Arpeggio
See Course Book No. 1 Page 28

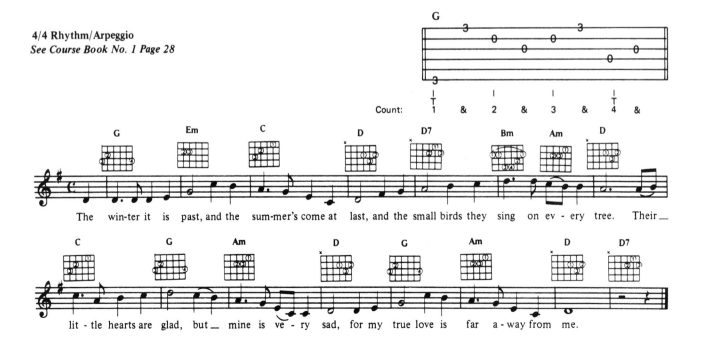

The win-ter it is past, and the sum-mer's come at last, and the small birds they sing on ev-ery tree. Their _____

lit-tle hearts are glad, but _ mine is ve-ry sad, for my true love is far a-way from me.

Verse 2

The rose the brier, by the water running clear
Give joy to the linnet and the bee
Their little hearts are blest, but mine is not at rest
While my true love is far away from me.

Verse 3

A livery I'll wear, and I'll comb down my hair
And in a velvet green I will appear
And straight I will repair to the Curragh of Kildare
For it's there I'll find some tidings of my dear.

Verse 4

I'll wear a cap of black, with a frill around my neck
Gold rings upon each finger will I wear
It's this I undertake, for my own true love's sake
She resides at the Curragh of Kildare.

Verse 5

My love is like the sun that in the firmament does run
And always proves constant and true
But hers is like the moon, that wanders up and down
And every month becomes something quite new.

Mary Hamilton Arranged Russ Shipton

6/8 Rhythm/Arpeggio
See Course Book No. 1 Page 28

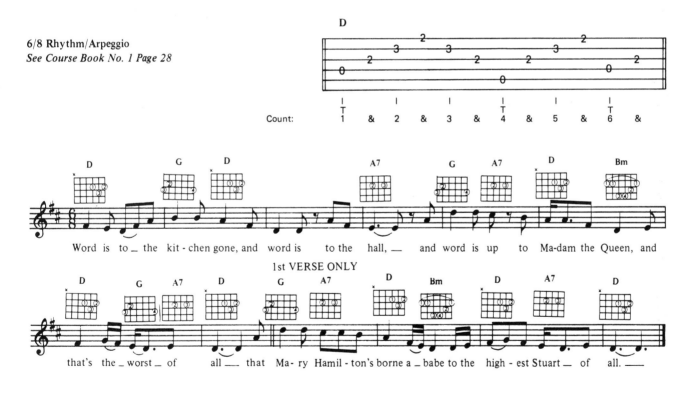

Word is to the kit-chen gone, and word is to the hall, — and word is up to Ma-dam the Queen, and

1st VERSE ONLY

that's the worst of all that Ma-ry Hamil-ton's borne a babe to the high-est Stuart of all.

Verse 2 (only the 1st verse has a third line)

Last night I dressed Queen Mary and put gold upon her hair
But now I've got for my reward the gallows to be my share.

Verse 3

Oh little did my mother think, the day she cradled me
The lands I was to travel in or the death I was to dee.

Verse 4

Last night there were four Marys, this night there'll be but three
There were Mary Beaton, and Mary Seaton, and Mary Carmichael and me.

Book 2

Tonight's The Night   Rod Stewart

4/4 Rhythm/Strumming/Swing
See Course Book No. 2 Page 3

VERSE

Stay a-way from my window. _ Stay a-way from my back door too. Disconnect the te - le - phone line.

Relax, baby, and draw that blind. Kick off your shoes, and sit right _ down, and loosen up that

pret-ty french gown. Let me pour you a good long drink, ooh, baby, don't you hesi - tate, 'cause to-night's the

night. It's gonna be all right, 'cause I love you girl, ain't no - bo - dy gonna stop us now!

Verse 2

Come on angel, my heart's on fire
Don't deny your man's desire
You'd be a fool to stop this tide
Spread your wings and let me come inside.

Don't say a word, my virgin child
Just let your inhibitions run wild
The secret is about to unfold
Upstairs before the night's too old.

Hush Little Baby   Arranged Russ Shipton

4/4 Rhythm/Strumming
See Course Book No. 2 Page 8

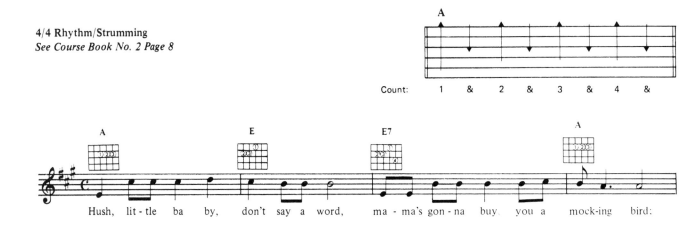

14

Hush, lit - tle ba - by, don't say a word, ma - ma's gon - na buy you a mock-ing bird:

if that mock-ing bird don't sing, ma-ma's gon-na buy you a dia-mond ring.

Verse 2
If that diamond ring turns brass
Mama's gonna buy you a looking glass
If that looking glass gets broke
Mama's gonna buy you a billy goat.

Verse 3
If that billygoat won't pull
Mama's gonna buy you a cart and bull
If that dart and bull turn over
Mama's gonna buy you a dog named Rover.

Verse 4
If that dog named Rover don't bark
Mama's gonna buy you a horse and cart
If that horse and cart fall down
You'll still be the sweetest girl in town.

© Copyright 1983 Dorsey Bros. Music, A Division of Music Sales Corp.
All Rights Reserved.   International Copyright Secured.

Dedicated Follower Of Fashion   Raymond Douglas Davies

Cut time Rhythm/Bass-strum
See Course Book No. 2 Page 9

VERSE

They seek him here,   they seek him _there.   His clothes are loud,   but ne-ver_ square.

It will make or break him so he's_ got to but the best, 'cos he's a ded-i-ca-ted fol-low-er of fash-ion. _

CHORUS

Oh yes he _ is (echo).   Oh yes he _ is (echo).   He thinks he is a flow-er_ to be looked at,

and when he pulls his fril-ly _ ny-lon pan-ties right up tight, he feels a ded-i-cat-ed fol-low-er of fash-ion. _

Verse 2
They seek him here
They seek him there
In Regent Street
And Leicester Square.
Everywhere the Carnabytion
Army marches on
Each one a dedicated follower
Of fashion.

Verse 3
And when he does
His little rounds
Round the boutiques
Of London Town
Eagerly pursuing
All the latest fads and trends
'Cause he's a dedicated follower
Of fashion.

Chorus (2)
Oh yes he is (oh yes he is)
Oh yes he is (oh yes he is)
There's one thing that he loves
And that is flattery
One week he's in polka dots
The next week he's in stripes
'Cause he's a dedicated follower
Of fashion.

Chorus 3
Oh yes he is (oh yes he is)
Oh yes he is (oh yes he is)
His world is built round
Discotheques and parties.
This pleasure-seeking individual
Always looks his best
'Cause he's a dedicated follower
Of fashion.

I Walk The Line   Johnny Cash

Cut time/Bass-strum
See Course Book No. 2 Page 10

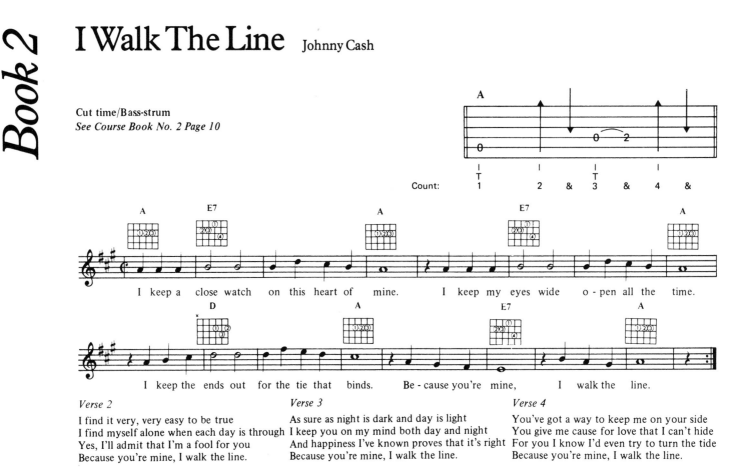

Count: 1   2 & 3 & 4 &

I keep a close watch on this heart of mine.   I keep my eyes wide o-pen all the time.

I keep the ends out for the tie that binds.   Be-cause you're mine,   I walk the line.

Verse 2

I find it very, very easy to be true
I find myself alone when each day is through
Yes, I'll admit that I'm a fool for you
Because you're mine, I walk the line.

Verse 3

As sure as night is dark and day is light
I keep you on my mind both day and night
And happiness I've known proves that it's right
Because you're mine, I walk the line.

Verse 4

You've got a way to keep me on your side
You give me cause for love that I can't hide
For you I know I'd even try to turn the tide
Because you're mine, I walk the line.

The First Time Ever I Saw Your Face   Ewan MacColl

4/4 Rhythm/Arpeggio
See Course Book No. 2 Page 15

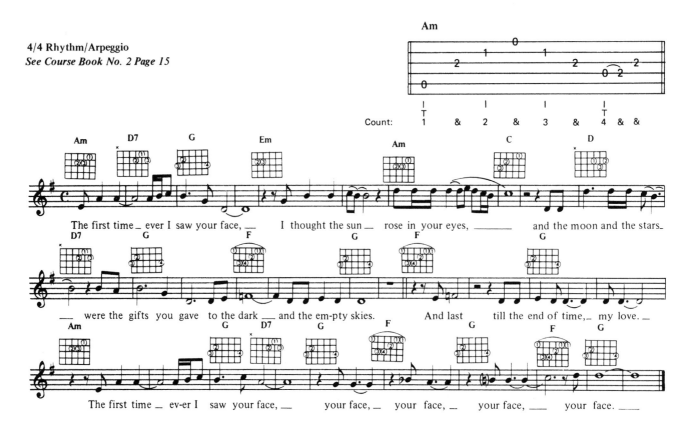

Count: 1 & 2 & 3 & 4 & &

The first time _ ever I saw your face, _   I thought the sun _ rose in your eyes, _____   and the moon and the stars_

_ were the gifts you gave to the dark _ and the em-pty skies.   And last   till the end of time,_ my love. _

The first time _ ev-er I saw your face, _   your face, _   your face, _   your face, ____   your face. ____

Verse 2 The first time ever I kissed your mouth
I felt the earth move in my hand
Like the trembling heart of a captive bird
That was there at my command, my love
That was there at my command.

Verse 3 The first time ever I lay with you
And felt your heart beat close to mine
I thought our joy would fill the earth
And last till the end of time, my love
And last till the end of time.

The House Carpenter Arranged Russ Shipton

Cut time/ Alternating thumb
See course Book No. 2 Page 22

"Well — met, well — met, my own true — love, well met, well met," cried he.

"I've just re‑turned from the salt, salt — sea, all for the love of thee." ___

Verse 2

Will you forsake your house carpenter
And come along with me?
I'll take you where the grass grows green
By the banks of the salt, salt sea.

Verse 3

Six ships, six ships all out on the sea
Seven more upon dry land
One hundred and ten, all brave sailor men
Will be at your command.

Verse 4

She picked up her own wee babe
And kisses gave him three
She said stay here with my house carpenter
And keep him good company.

Verse 5

Well they'd not been gone but about two weeks
I know it was not three
When this fair lady began to weep
She wept most bitterly.

Verse 6

I do not weep for my house carpenter
Or for any golden store
But I do weep for my own wee babe
Who I shall never see any more.

Verse 7

Well they'd not been gone but about three weeks
I'm sure it was not four
Our gallant ship sprung a leak and sank
Never to rise any more.

Duncan Paul Simon

Cut Time/Alternating thumb
See Course Book No. 2 Page 22

Couple in the next room   bound to win a prize,– they've been goin' at it all — night   long.   Well I'm tryin' to get some

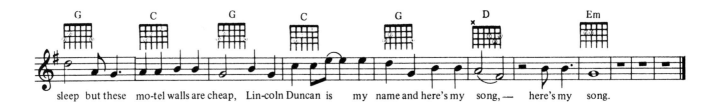

sleep but these mo-tel walls are cheap, Lin-coln Duncan is my name and here's my song, — here's my song.

Verse 2

My father was a fisherman, my mamma was a fisherman's
                                                    friend
And I was born in the boredom and the chowder
So when I reached my prime
I left my home in the Maritimes
Headed down the turnpike for New England
Sweet New England.

Verse 3

Holes in my confidence, holes in the knees of my jeans
I's left without a penny in my pocket
Oo hoo hoo wee
I's about as destituted as a kid could be
And I wished I wore a ring so I could hock it
I'd like to hock it.

Verse 4

A young girl in a parking lot was preaching to a crowd
Singin' sacred songs and readin' from the bible
Well, I told her I was lost
And she told me all about the Pentecost
And I seen that girl as the road to my survival.

Verse 5

Just later on the very same night
When I crept to her tent with a flashlight
And my long years of innocence ended
Well, she took me to the woods
Sayin' "Here comes somethin' and it feels so good!"
And just like a dog, I was befriended
I was befriended.

Verse 6

Oh, oh, what a night, oh what a garden of delight
Even now that sweet memory lingers
I was playin' my guitar
Lyin' underneath the stars
Just thankin' the Lord for my fingers
For my fingers.

Lady D'Arbanville   Cat Stevens

Cut time/Alternating thumb
See Course Book No. 2 Page 24

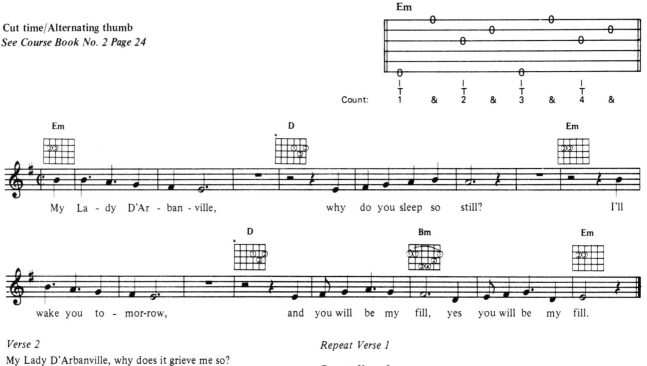

My La - dy D'Ar - ban - ville, why do you sleep so still? I'll

wake you to - mor-row, and you will be my fill, yes you will be my fill.

Verse 2

My Lady D'Arbanville, why does it grieve me so?
But your heart seems so silent, why do you breathe so low?
Why do you breathe so low?

Repeat Verse 1

Verse 3

My Lady D'Arbanville, you look so cold tonight
Your lips feel like winter, your skin has turned to white
Your skin has turned to white.

Repeat Verse 1

Repeat Verse 2

Verse 4

I loved you my lady, though in your grave you lie
I'll always be with you, this rose will never die
This rose will never die.

18

Coat Of Many Colours Dolly Parton

Cut time/Alternating thumb
See Course Book No. 2 Page 22

Count: 1 2 & 3 & 4

INTRO.

Back through the years I go wand'ring once a-gain, __ back to the sea-sons of my youth. I re-call a box of rags that some-one gave us, and how my mama put the rags to use. There were rags of man-y co-lours but ev'-ry piece was small, and I did-n't have a coat __ and it was way down in the fall. __ Ma-ma sewed the rags to get-her, sewing

CHORUS

ev'-ry piece with love. __ She made my coat of man-y co-lours, that I was so proud of. (2. As she) My coat of man-y co-lours that my ma-ma made for me, made on-ly from rags, but I wore it so proud-ly. _____ Al-though we had no money, I was rich as I could be, in my coat of man-y co-lours my ma-ma made for me. ___(3. So with)

Verse 2

As she sewed, she told a story from the bible she had read
About a coat of many colours Joseph wore, and then she said
"Perhaps this coat will bring you good luck and happiness"
And I just couldn't wait to wear it and mama blessed it with a kiss.

Verse 3

So with patches on my britches and holes in both my shoes
In my coat of many colours I hurried off to school
Just to find the others laughing and a-making fun of me
In my coat of many colours my mama made for me.

Verse 4

And oh I couldn't understand it, for I felt I was rich
And I told them of the love my mama sewed in every stitch
And I told them all the story mama told me while she sewed
And how my coat of many colours was worth more than all their clothes.

2nd Chorus

But they didn't understand it, and I tried to make them see
That one is only poor, if they choose to be
Now I know we had no money, but I was as rich as I could be
In my coat of many colours my mama made for me.

19

The Ferryman Ralph McTell

4/4 Rhythm/Alternating thumb
See Course Book No. 2 Page 24

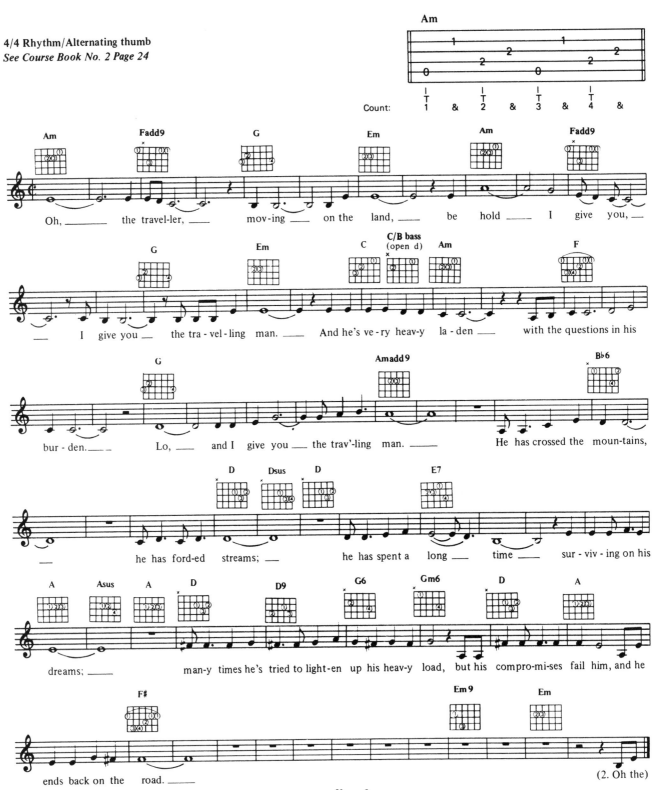

Oh, _____ the travel-ler, _____ mov-ing _____ on the land, _____ be hold _____ I give you, _____ I give you _____ the tra - vel-ling man. _____ And he's ve-ry heav-y la - den _____ with the questions in his bur - den. _____ Lo, _____ and I give you _____ the trav'-ling man. _____ He has crossed the moun-tains, he has ford-ed streams; _____ he has spent a long _____ time _____ sur - viv-ing on his dreams; _____ man-y times he's tried to light-en up his heav-y load, but his compro-mi-ses fail him, and he ends back on the road. _____

(2. Oh the)

Verse 2

Oh the traveller he is weary, the travelling man is tired
For the road is never ending, in his fear he has cried
Aloud for a saviour and in vain for a teacher
Someone to lighten up the load
And he's heard the sounds of war in a gentle shower of rain
And the whisperings of despair that he could not explain
The reason for his journey or the reason it began
Or was there any reason for the travelling man?

Verse 3

At last he reached a river so beautiful and wide
But the current was so strong he could not reach the other side
And the weary travelling man looked for a ferryman
Strong enough to row against the tide
And the ferryman was old but he moved the boat so well
Or did the river move the boat, the traveller could not tell
Said the ferryman "You're weary, and the answers that you seek
Are in the singing river, listen humbly it will speak."

Verse 4

Oh the traveller closed his eyes and he listened and he heard
Only the river murmuring and the beating of his heart
Then he heard the river laughing and he heard the river crying
And in it was the beauty and the sadness of the world
And he heard the sounds of dying but he heard the sounds of birth
And slowly his ears heard all the sounds on earth
The sounds blended together and they became a whole
And the rhythm was his heartbeat to the music in his soul.

Verse 5

And the river had no beginning as it flowed into the seas
And the seas filled the clouds and the rains filled the streams
And as slowly as the sunrise he opened up his eyes
To find the ferryman had gone, the boat moved gently on the tide
And the river flowed within him and with it he was one
And the seas moved round the earth and the earth around the sun
And the traveller was the river, was the boat and ferryman
Was the journey and the song that the singing river sang.

My Sweet Lord   George Harrison

4/4 Rhythm/Strumming
See Course Book No. 3 Page 4

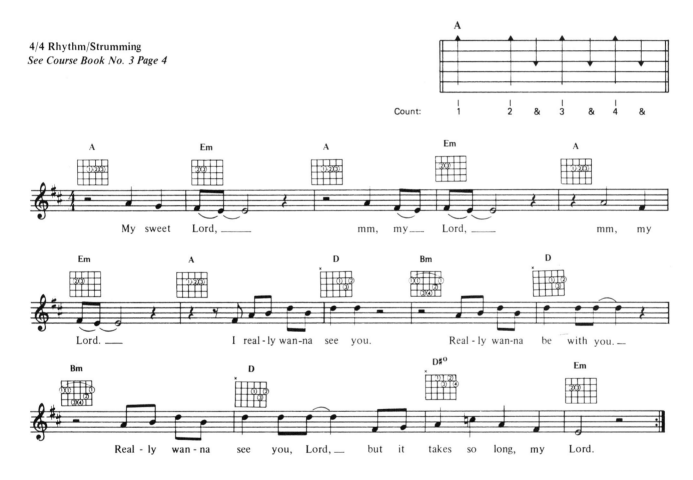

My sweet Lord, _____ mm, my___ Lord, _____ mm, my

Lord. ___ I real-ly wan-na see you. Real-ly wan-na be with you. _

Real-ly wan-na see you, Lord, _ but it takes so long, my Lord.

Verse 2

My sweet Lord
Mm my Lord
Mm my Lord.
I really want to know you
Really want to go with you
Really want to show you Lord
That it won't take long my Lord.

Verse 3

My sweet Lord
Mm my Lord
Mm my Lord.
I really want to see you
Really want to see you
Really want to see you Lord
But it takes so long my Lord.

Candle In The Wind

Elton John & Bernie Taupin

Cut time Rhythm/Strumming
See Course Book No. 3 Page 6

VERSE

Good-bye Norma Jean, though I nev-er knew you at all, you had the grace to hold your- self, while

those a - round __ you crawled. They crawled out of the wood -work, and they whispered

in to your brain. They set you on a tread-mill, and they made you change your name. And it

CHORUS

seems to me __ you lived your life like a can - dle in __ the wind, ne - ver know-ing who to cling to when the

rain set in. __ And I would have __ liked to have known you, but I was just a kid. __ Your

can - dle burnt out long be - fore __ your le - gend ev - er did.

Verse 2

Loneliness was tough, the toughest role you ever played
Hollywood created a superstar and pain was the price you paid.
Even when you died the press still hounded you
All the papers had to say was that Marilyn was found in the nude.

Verse 3

Goodbye, Norma Jean, though I never knew you at all
You had the grace to hold yourself while those around you crawled.
Goodbye, Norma Jean, from the young man in the twenty-second row
Who sees you as something more than sexual
More than just our Marilyn Monroe.

Save The Last Dance For Me
Doc Pomus & Mort Shuman

Cut time/Strumming
See Course Book No. 3 Page 6

Count: 1 & 2 & 3 & 4 &
(spread strum)

VERSE

You can dance ev'-ry dance with the guy who gave you the eye, let him hold you tight. _ You can

smile ev'-ry smile for the man who held your hand 'neath the pale moon-light, _ but don't for-

get who's tak-ing you home, and in whose arms you're gon-na be. So dar-ling, _ save the

MIDDLE SECTION

last dance for me! Ba-by don't you know I love you so? _ can't you feel it when we touch?

(stop)

I will ne-ver, ne-ver let you go: _ I love you oh so much.

Verse 2

Oh I know that the music is fine
Like sparkling wine, go and have your fun
Laugh and sing, but while we're apart
Don't give your heart to anyone
'Cause don't forget who's taking you home
And in whose arms you're gonna be
So darling, save the last dance for me.

Verse 3

You can dance, go and carry on
Till the night is gone, and it's time to go
If he asks if you're all alone
Can he take you home, you must tell him no
'Cause don't forget who's taking you home
And in whose arms you're gonna be
So darling, save the last dance for me.

The Nightingale

Arranged Russ Shipton

3/4 Rhythm/Arpeggio (fast)

See Course Book No. 3 Page 14

Verse 2

From out of his knapsack he took a fine fiddle
And he played her such merry tunes that you ever did hear
And he played her such merry tunes that the valley did ring
And they both sat down together love to hear the nightingale sing.

Verse 3

Oh soldier, oh soldier, will you marry me?
Oh no said the soldier that can never be
For I have my own wife at home in my own counteree
And she is the sweetest little thing that you ever did see.

Verse 4

Now I'm off to India for seven long years
Drinking wines and strong whiskey instead of cool beers
And if ever I return again it will be in the spring
And we'll both sit down together love to hear the nightingale sing.

Hey That's No Way To Say Goodbye
Leonard Cohen

4/4 Rhythm/Bass-pinch
See Course Book No. 3 Page 20

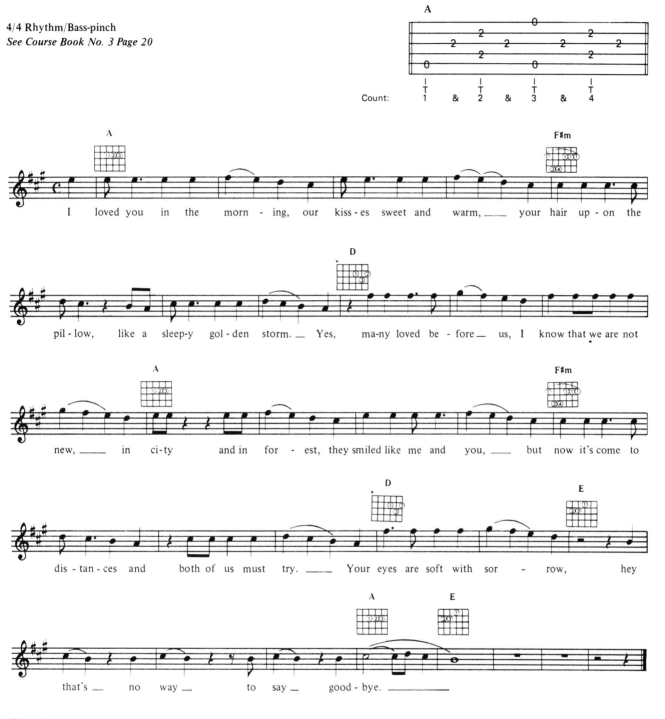

I loved you in the morn - ing, our kiss - es sweet and warm, ___ your hair up - on the

pil - low, like a sleep - y gol - den storm. ___ Yes, ma - ny loved be - fore ___ us, I know that we are not

new, ___ in ci - ty and in for - est, they smiled like me and you, ___ but now it's come to

dis - tan - ces and both of us must try. ___ Your eyes are soft with sor - row, hey

that's ___ no way ___ to say ___ good - bye. ___

Verse 2
I'm not looking for another as I wander in my time
Walk me to the corner, our steps will always rhyme
You know my love goes with you as your love stays with me
It's just the way it changes, like the shoreline and the sea
But let's not talk of love or chains and things we can't untie
Your eyes are soft with sorrow
Hey, that's no way to say goodbye.

Repeat 1st 4 lines of V. 1 and last 3 lines of V. 2.

Terminus   Ralph McTell

4/4 Rhythm/Bass-pinch
See Course Book No. 3 Page 20

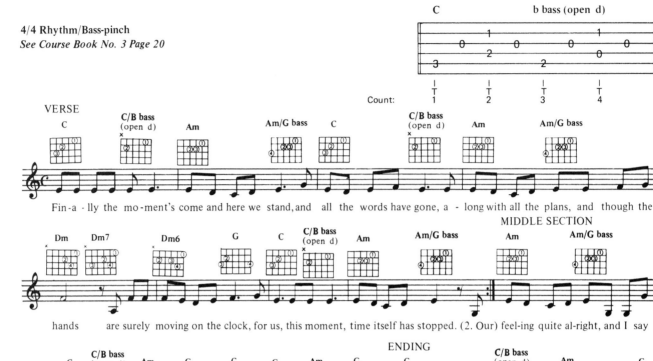

VERSE

Fin-a-lly the mo-ment's come and here we stand, and all the words have gone, a - long with all the plans, and though the

MIDDLE SECTION

hands   are surely moving on the clock, for us, this moment, time itself has stopped. (2. Our) feel-ing quite al-right, and I say

ENDING

"Yes."   through the door marked "exit," in - to the world outside.

Verse 2

Our early morning eyes still feel a little sore
And bodies sweetly aching from the night before
I can feel the cold platform through my shoes
There must be someting to be said, but what's the use?

Verse 3

The wind picks up some paper and blows it past our feet
We watch it, grateful that our eyes don't have to meet
A screaming whistle rips the air
And takes away the last seconds we have shared.

Verse 4

In still photographs the train begins its run
And suddenly all the words I should have said suddenly have come
Someone touches me and asks me for a light
And wonders if I'm feeling quite alright
And I say "Yes."

Verse 5

On another platform, there stands a train
The same old scene is to be shot again
The wind picks up some paper and with it I shall ride
Out through the door marked "Exit", into the world outside.

Here There And Everywhere   John Lennon & Paul McCartney

Cut time/Bass-pinch and strumming mixed
See Course Book No. 4 Page 4

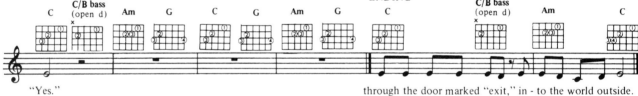

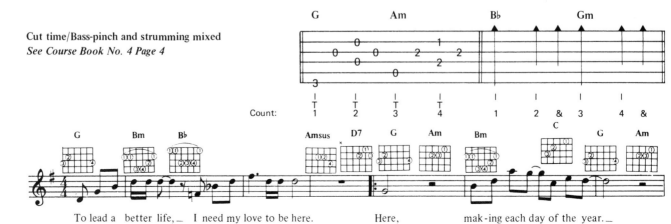

To lead a better life,_ I need my love to be here.   Here,   mak-ing each day of the year._

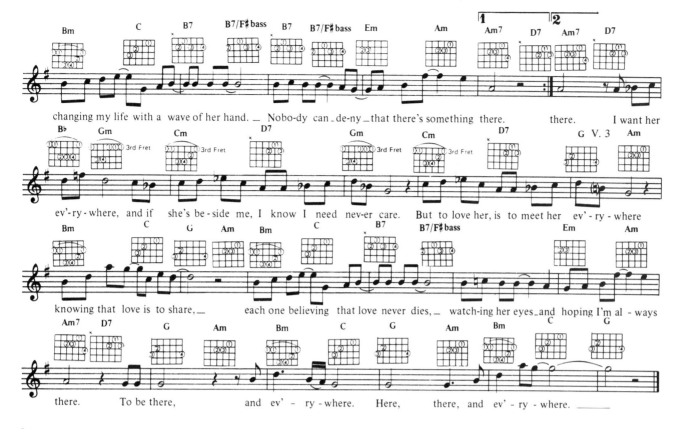

| Bm | C | B7 | B7/F♯ bass | B7 | B7/F♯ bass | Em | Am | Am7 D7 | Am7 D7 |

changing my life with a wave of her hand. ___ Nobo-dy can de-ny ___ that there's something there. ___ there. I want her

| B♭ | Gm | Cm | D7 | Gm | Cm | D7 | G V. 3 | Am |

ev'-ry-where, and if she's be-side me, I know I need nev-er care. But to love her, is to meet her ev'-ry-where

| Bm | C | G | Am | Bm | C | B7 | B7/F♯ bass | Em | Am |

knowing that love is to share, ___ each one believing that love never dies, ___ watch-ing her eyes ___ and hoping I'm al - ways

| Am7 D7 | G | Am | Bm | C | G | Am | Bm | C | G |

there. To be there, and ev' - ry - where. Here, there, and ev' - ry - where. ___

Rivers Of Babylon Farian, Reyam, Dowe & McMaughton

4/4 Rhythm/Strumming/Damping
See Course Book No. 4 Page 9

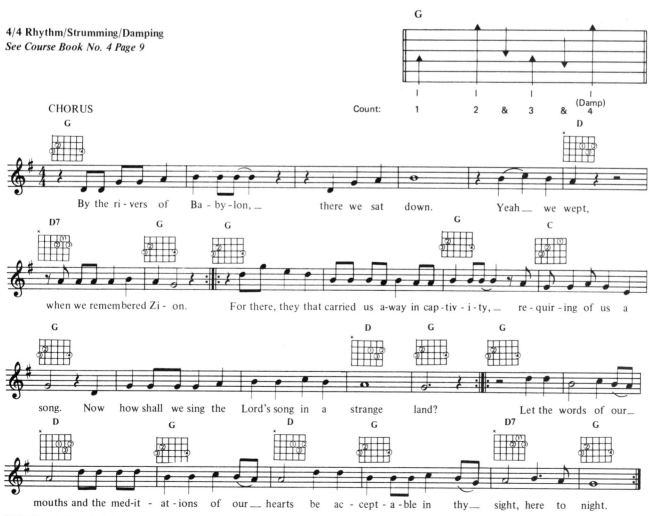

| | | | G | | |

CHORUS
| G | | | | | D |

By the ri - vers of Ba - by - lon, ___ there we sat down. Yeah ___ we wept,

| D7 | G | G | | G | C |

when we remembered Zi - on. For there, they that carried us a-way in cap-tiv-i-ty, ___ re - quir-ing of us a

| G | | | D | G | G |

song. Now how shall we sing the Lord's song in a strange land? Let the words of our ___

| D | G | D | G | D7 | G |

mouths and the med-it - at - ions of our ___ hearts be ac-cept-a-ble in thy ___ sight, here to night.

Father And Son Cat Stevens

Book 4

Cut time/Strumming
See Course Book No. 4 Page 14

(Father) It's not time to make a change, just re-lax take it eas-y, you're still young, that's your fault, there's so much you have to know. Find a girl, set-tle down, if you want, you can marry; look at me, I am old, but I'm hap-py. I was once like you are now, and I know that it's not eas-y to be calm when you've found something go-ing on. But take your time, think a lot, think of every-thing you've got, for you will still be here to-morrow but your dreams may not!

(Son) How can I try, to ex-plain? When I do he turns a-way a-gain. It's al-ways been the same, same old sto-ry. From the moment I could talk, I was ordered to lis-ten, now there's a way, — and I know that I have to go a-way. I know I have to go!

(2. It's not)

Verse 3 (Son)
All the times that I've cried, keeping all the things I knew inside
It's hard, but it's harder to ignore it
If they were right, I'd agree, but it's them they know, not me
Now there's a way, and I know that I have to go away
I know I have to go.

Squeaker's Prowl Russ Shipton

4/4 Rhythm/Alternating thumb/Swing
See Course Book No. 4 Page 10

On The Run Russ Shipton

4/4 Rhythm/Alternating Thumb/Hammer-ons and pull-offs
See Course Book No. 4 Page 13.

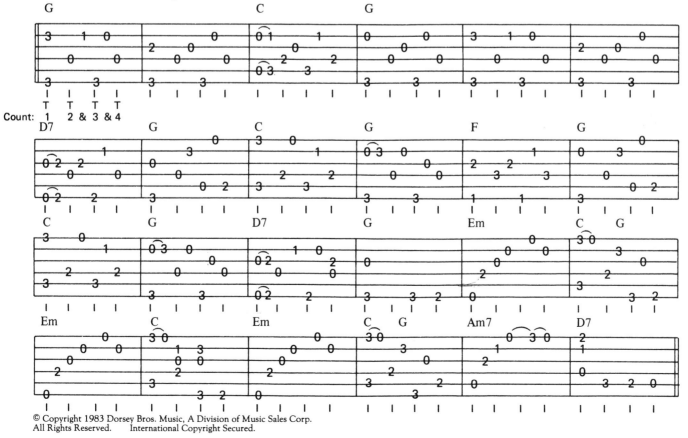

Flight Of The Frisbee Russ Shipton

Book 4

3/4 Rhythm/Alternating thumb/Swing
See Course Book No. 4 Page 14

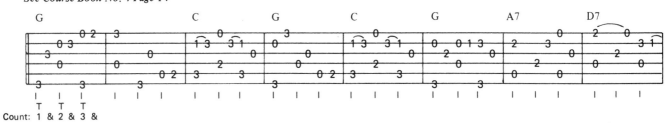

Count: 1 & 2 & 3 &

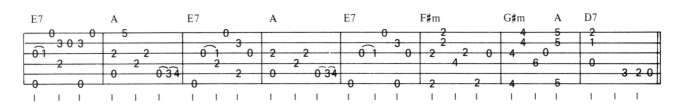

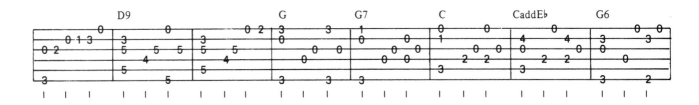

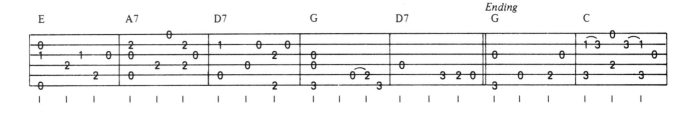

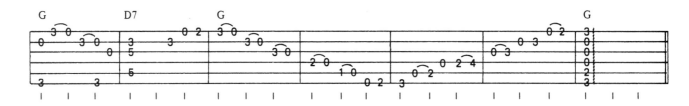

Rag Of Yer Own Russ Shipton

4/4 Rhythm/Alternating thumb & variations/Swing
See Course Book No. 4 Page 10

Section 1

Thursday's Theme Russ Shipton

3/4 Rhythm/Arpeggio
See Course Book No. 4 Page 4

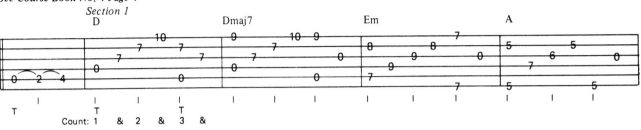

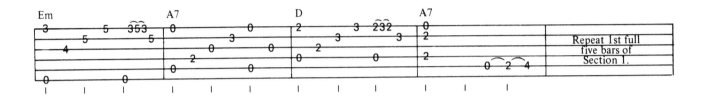

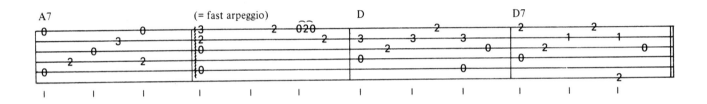

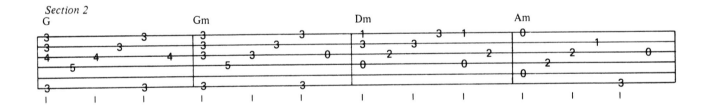

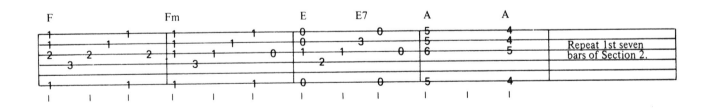

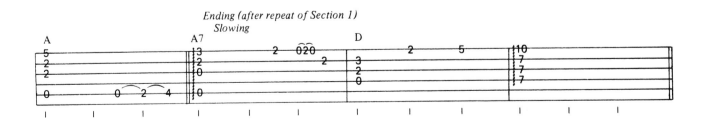

Campbell's Jig Russ Shipton

4/4 Rhythm/Monotonic Bass/Swing
See Course Book No. 4 Page 15

Section 1

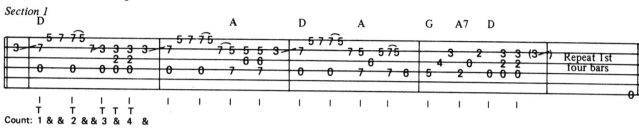

Count: 1 & & 2 & & 3 & 4 &

Section 2

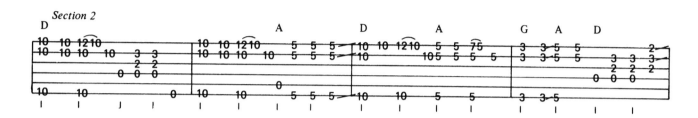

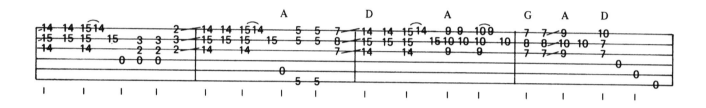

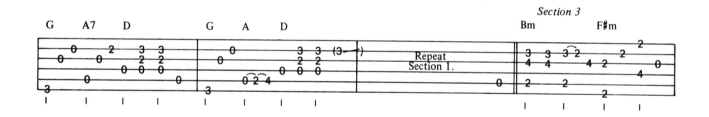

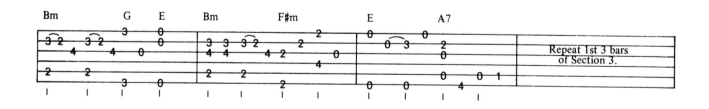

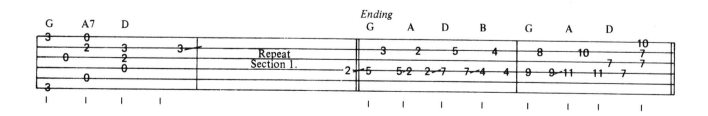

Weekend Shuffle Russ Shipton

4/4 Rhythm/Alternating thumb/Swing
See Course Book No. 4 Page 14

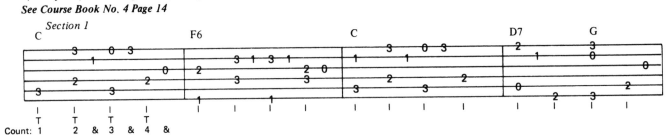

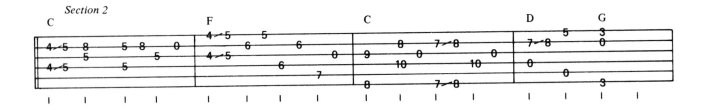

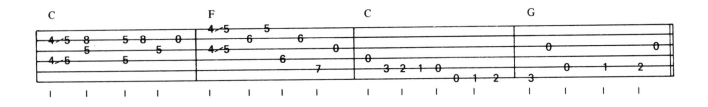

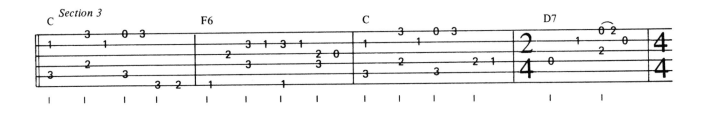

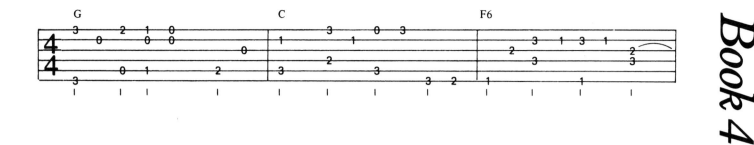

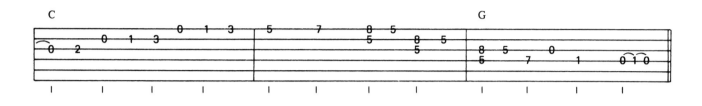

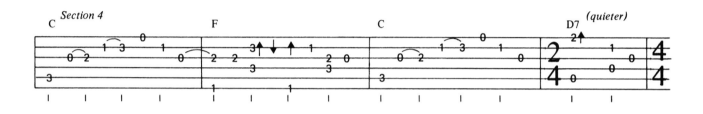

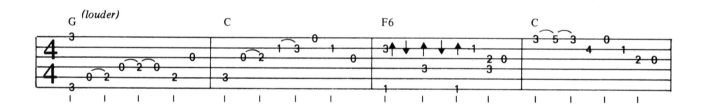

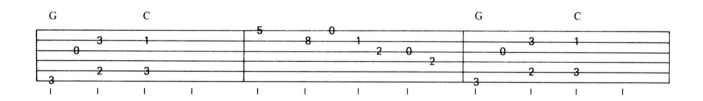

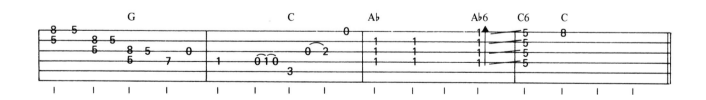

Book 4

T.T.'s Blues Russ Shipton

4/4 Rhythm/Montonic Bass/Swing
See Course Book No. 4 Page 15

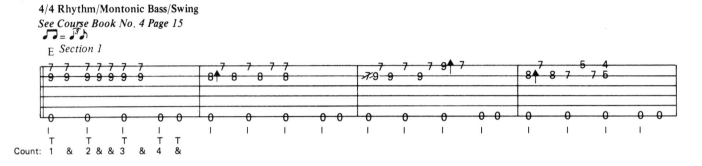

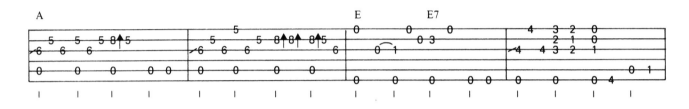

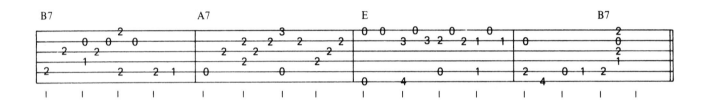

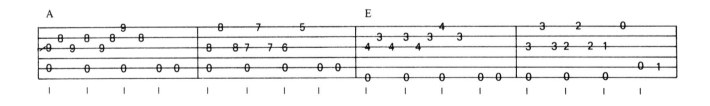

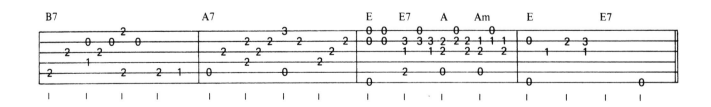

Marathon Mania Arranged Russ Shipton

4/4 Rhythm/Alternating thumb/fast
See Course Book No. 4 Page 16

Section 1

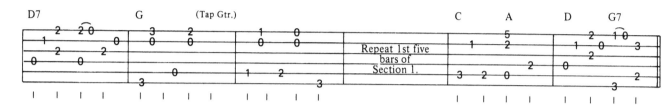

Count: 1 & 2 & 3 4 &

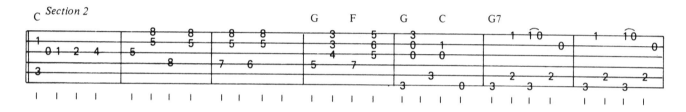

Section 2

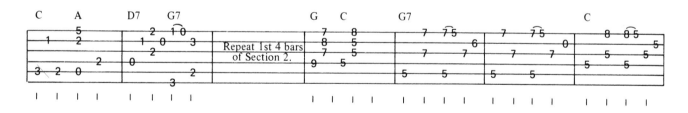

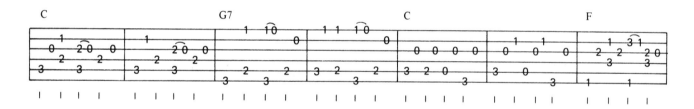

(to 1st Section)

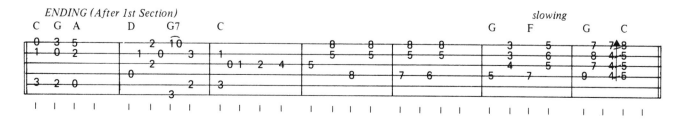

ENDING (After 1st Section)

Rollerball Russ Shipton

Book 4

4/4 Right Hand/Alternating/Thumb
See Course Book No. 4 Page 16

Intro:

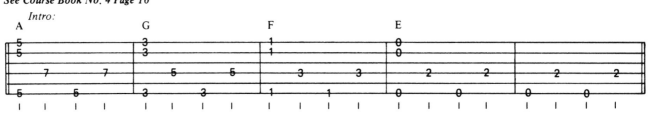

Section 1

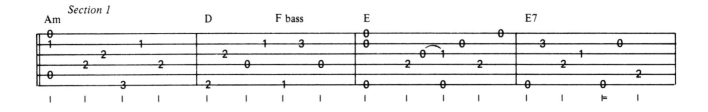

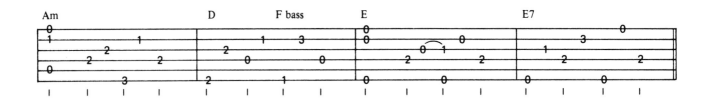

Section 2

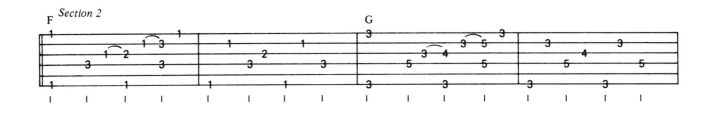

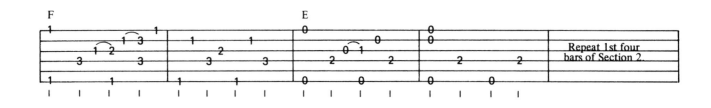

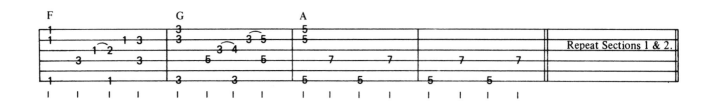

38

Two-Step Promenade   Russ Shipton

4/4 Rhythm/Monotonic Bass/Slides/Swing
See Course Book No. 4 Page 18

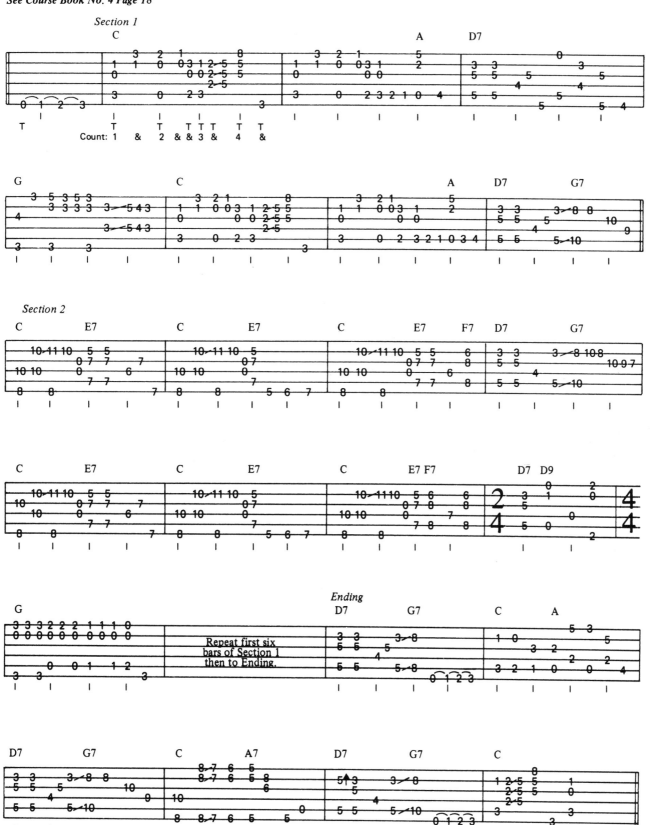